"Without question, in my 14 years as quarterback for the Pittsburgh Steelers, Elvin Bethea was the one player that we focused on to plan our offensive game plan around. He disrupted our entire game plan, and he was the only player ever to do that. Elvin was the one player we could never control. I have the greatest respect and admiration for Elvin Bethea."

—TERRY BRADSHAW
Pittsburgh Steelers
Hall of Fame 1989

"Elvin Bethea was not only an outstanding defensive end, but an outstanding team leader. I didn't look forward to playing against him, but I thoroughly enjoyed our time as teammates."

—ARCHIE MANNING
New Orleans Saints
1978 NFC MVP

"Whenever we played the Houston Oilers, there was always one defensive player we had to account for—and that player was Elvin Bethea. The entire game plan—run plays and pass protection—was set up with Elvin in mind. He was always a big pain in the neck!"

—BOB GRIESE
Miami Dolphins
Hall of Fame 1990

"Don't let that charming smile fool you. This guy was an assassin. There was nothing dirty about Elvin, but he was relentless. You had to sit on him until the play was over because there was just no let-up."

—*LEN DAWSON*
Kansas City Chiefs
Hall of Fame 1987

"I became Elvin's teammate during his 15th NFL season. I could not believe his quickness, his work ethic, and his love for the game. Elvin Bethea showed me what it took to be a professional."

—*MIKE MUNCHAK*
Houston Oilers
Hall of Fame 2001

"We always had to be concerned about Elvin Bethea when we were game-planning because of the enormous talent he brought against the run and rushing the passer. When I coached him in the Pro Bowls, he was a joy to work with. Elvin was the kind of guy you had to have on a team to win."

—*CHUCK NOLL*
Pittsburgh Steelers
Hall of Fame 1993

"Regardless of the score, Elvin Bethea had but one speed—*full*. He was as wide as he was tall so it was like throwing yourself in front of a wrecking ball. Our games usually started out as boxing matches but soon deteriorated into a WWE wrestling match. The thing that separated Elvin from many of the rest was that we always shook hands after the game. We always acknowledged that we both played as hard as we could and respected each other's efforts on the field of battle. Elvin Bethea was not only one of the best—he was also one of the classiest."

—*DOUG DIEKEN*
Cleveland Browns
All-Pro 1980

"When we played the Steelers, if I was knocked down, Elvin made sure that Terry Bradshaw was knocked down, too. At first, I thought it was just a coincidence, but after awhile, I realized Elvin was sticking up for a teammate and letting the Steelers know that whatever happened to me was going to happen to Bradshaw."

—*DAN PASTORINI*
Houston Oilers
Pro Bowl 1976

"Elvin Bethea is one of the nicest people you could ever want to know. There's nothing phony about him. What you see is what you get. It took him too long to get into the Hall of Fame, but there's no doubt he deserves to be there."

—*LEROY KELLY*
Cleveland Browns
Hall of Fame 1994

Smashmouth

My Football Journey from Trenton to Canton

Elvin Bethea
with Mark Adams

Foreword by
Bum Phillips

www.SportsPublishingLLC.com

ISBN: 1-58261-881-X

Publishers: Peter L. Bannon and Joseph J. Bannon Sr.
Senior managing editor: Susan M. Moyer
Acquisitions editor: Dean Reinke
Developmental editor: Elisa Bock Laird
Art director: K. Jeffrey Higgerson
Dust jacket design: Kenneth J. O'Brien
Project manager: Jim Henehan
Photo editor: Erin Linden-Levy
Vice president of sales and marketing: Kevin King
Media and promotions managers: Mike Hagan (regional),
        Randy Fouts (national), Maurey Williamson (print)

Printed in the United States of America

Sports Publishing L.L.C.
804 North Neil Street
Champaign, IL 61820

Phone: 1-877-424-2665
Fax: 217-363-2073
www.SportsPublishingLLC.com

To my parents, Henrietta and Jesse Bethea, who taught me that hard work was the way to achieve anything of great value. I thank them for their support and encouragement over the years, including countless rides to practice in all kinds of weather and all their care packages, which got me through the lean years of college. I survived!!!

To my children, LaMonte, Brittany, and Damon—I LOVE YOU ALL!

To my wife, Pat, for all your love and support—"Who loves ya, baby?"

Finally—to all of my family, friends, and especially the true Houston Oiler fans who supported me and our teams through the good times and the bad—"Luv Ya Blue!"

—Elvin Bethea

Contents

Foreword

When I was Sid Gillman's defensive assistant for the San Diego Chargers in the early 1970s, I got to see a lot of Elvin Bethea from the other side of the field. He seemed huge. Our offensive plan was to run at him and double-team him, but he was so quick, he could just flip around a double team and get to whoever had the ball at that moment. When I came to the Oilers with Gillman in 1974, I didn't anticipate Elvin being as small as he was. He only weighed about 245 to 250, and he wasn't really physically impressive in person—until he started playing football.

Elvin Bethea got off the ball quicker than anybody in the league. He was simply one of the most outstanding defensive players in the league for a long time, but he didn't get recognized for that because the Oilers were so awful for so long. Elvin played every down at full speed right down to the whistle. One of the reasons he couldn't keep his weight up into the 260s was because he always worked it off! He'd chase down players with the speed and agility of a running back and catch them from behind. He was an outstanding pass rusher and equally outstanding on run defense. Whatever we asked him to do, Elvin got it done.

If there's one thing that any coach of Elvin Bethea's will say about him, it's that he practiced as hard as he played. His work ethic was second to none. He got there early, stayed late, and was a genuine student of the game. You see, Elvin enjoyed football. Anybody who enjoys practice *really* enjoys football. A lot of great players don't enjoy practice or even practice very hard, but Elvin was an excellent practice player, and he loved it. One of the greatest compliments that opposing teams paid him was to double-team him regularly. They had to, actually, otherwise they'd get killed. He also burned opposing offenses with his ability to diagnose plays so well. Elvin would head right for the cutoff spot every time and, with his quickness, that meant lights out for the running back who thought there'd be a hole for him.

When I was coaching Elvin Bethea, I felt I was coaching a guy as good as any of those who got into the Hall of Fame. He belonged in the same class as Joe Greene, but he didn't get the publicity. Greene got into the Hall of Fame on his first try, and Elvin was as dominant for us as Joe was for Pittsburgh. Elvin just wouldn't come out of a game. He would play with pain. Everybody respected Elvin, and, just as important, they liked him. He had a confidence that a lot of people aren't blessed with. He was fun in the clubhouse, he was fun on the team bus, he was fun off the field, he was fun on the field—well, maybe not fun *on* the field. I was relieved when Elvin finally made the Hall of Fame. The wait was just awful. By the time his sixth, seventh, eighth, ninth, and 10th years of eligibility rolled by, they were putting in younger guys, and the voters seemed to forget about him. Something that those Hall of Fame voters may have forgotten over the years is that Elvin Bethea is the kind of guy you have to have on your team to win. You've got to have one guy who's better than any guy they've got. Elvin was that guy for the Oilers. He didn't just tell other players what to do; he showed them what to do. To your defense, he's everything. This book will take you inside his head and behind the scenes of his unique football journey. I'm happy to have been part of the ride with him.

—*Bum Phillips*
Goliad, Texas
March 24, 2005

Acknowledgments

The authors gratefully acknowledge the following people for their invaluable contributions to this book:

- Terry Bradshaw (and his agent, David Gershenson), Len Dawson, Doug Dieken, Bob Griese, Leroy Kelly, Archie Manning, Chuck Noll, Dan Pastorini, Bum Phillips, Billy Shaw, and Mike Munchak for their generous and full-hearted comments.

- Adam Bethea and Abraham Carey for photo research and acquisition.

- Our wives, Pat Bethea and Rachel Long, for their love, support, and encouragement.

- Joyce Palmer, Susan Gilbert, and Jack Westin for their assistance and consultation.

- Bob Hulsey for providing clarity on some important events in the Houston Oiler timeline.

- Jim Hackett for the authors photo on the dust jacket.

- Bob Hyde for Oiler photo research.

- Elisa Bock Laird, our unflappable editor at Sports Publishing L.L.C., for her considerable patience, professionalism, and positive attitude.

Chapter 1

FROM TRENTON...

Trenton, New Jersey, is my hometown. Nothing will ever change that. Of course, Houston is my home now, and it has been for more than 30 years. These years in Houston have been the happiest, most fulfilling of my life, and I wouldn't trade what I've had here for anything. But none of this changes the fact that Trenton will always be "home" for me. I don't get back to Trenton very often, maybe only once or twice a year, and there was even a time when I swore I'd *never* go back. You'll certainly never see me living in Trenton again (unless they put a dome over it and heat it throughout those brutal winters). However, my affection for my hometown runs deep and wide. Actually, let's call it a love-hate relationship.

My mother, Henrietta Carey, came from Snow Hill, Maryland, but she met my father, Jesse James Bethea, in New Jersey. He was from Dillon, South Carolina. When they first met, my mother was attending Apex College in Trenton, and my father was a laborer in one of the big factories in the industrial part of southern New Jersey. He had been a military policeman during World War II, and even though he swears that he saw action, I'm convinced he never left Fort Dix. (Well, at least he helped keep the Nazis from invading New Jersey.) My parents were married after the war, but not before I was born on March 1, 1946. Because they weren't married, I was born Elvin Carey, and I didn't officially become Elvin Bethea until my birth certificate was amended 13 years later.

My father was a simple man who believed in hard work. Every Christmas he asked for an orange and some RED MAN tobacco, and that was all he needed. Chewing tobacco was probably his only recreation. No movies, no sports, no card games, no fishing—just work. I do remember that he enjoyed listening to the radio on Sunday nights. That was the night for *The Amos 'N Andy Show,* but otherwise he lived to work. My father was about six foot three and weighed in at about 270 to 280 pounds, but he always seemed like a giant to me. He used his incredible strength, and his unwavering work ethic, to put food on the table.

My mother was a big-boned woman and was not short for a lady in those days (probably about five foot seven or eight). She was easy-going, laid back, and never seemed to get upset about anything. She was a very religious woman and always seemed to be helping someone. Mom was always out in the neighborhood giving an extra hand to somebody who needed it, and she was always trying to make life better for someone else. She was stern at times, though. She controlled the kids until it got to be too much, and then my father stepped in. She never took the discipline as far as Dad did, but she definitely got her point across. Her lifelong motto, which she instilled in all of us, was "Just be yourself."

I was the first of nine children for Henrietta and Jesse, and life in the Bethea household was never dull because there was always something to do. Our house was big but far from luxurious. My room was about 10 feet by seven feet and barely big enough to turn around in. As the old joke goes, my room was so small that I had to step outside to change my mind. I shared this room with one of my brothers until I was nearly 17. We had to stick a piece of rag or toilet paper into the holes in the screen during the summer or we'd get eaten alive by mosquitoes. My three sisters were in another small room, and my parents were in the master bedroom. Eventually, my parents added four more kids to the mix, but the house never got bigger!

Our house sat on four acres in the rural portion of Lawrence Township and had no running water and, therefore, no indoor plumbing. We also had a one-and-a-half seat outhouse that functioned as our toilet. The half seat was for the kids, and we had to grow into using the full seat. Also when the outhouse got too full,

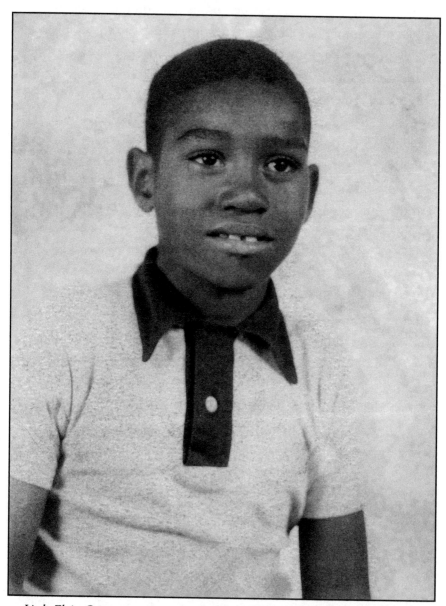

Little Elvin Carey at age 8, soon to be Elvin Bethea. **Photo courtesy of Elvin Bethea**

we just covered it up and dug another one. I suppose that's why they call New Jersey "The Garden State." Even after we got an indoor toilet just before I left for college, I still had to cart the five-gallon buckets of water needed to flush it. There was a pond about 50 yards away across the street from the house. One of my least favorite chores was to lug buckets of water back to the house from that pond to fill a 50-gallon oil drum that we used for our bathing and toilet flushing water. When the pond was frozen in the winter, I just broke the ice until I got to some liquid.

As parents of nine, my mother and father were very strict disciplinarians. We got some fine beatings if we disobeyed an order or slacked on our chores. If we didn't mop the floors or wash the dishes when we were told, we got it good with the cord of the electric iron, which left welts. I didn't count the strokes in those beatings, I just ran. One time I was deep in sleep under the safe, warm covers of my bed when I was awakened by the sharp sting of the ironing cord as it hit my body. I had been told to do a chore before I went to bed that night and I had forgotten to do it. My father decided to issue a wakeup call. My mother didn't slack off, either—she used a belt. Today, they would probably be put in jail for some of those beatings, but we survived them and haven't seemed to suffer any ill effects.

The best thing I can say about being the oldest of nine was that I had the first crack at the clothes. When I outgrew something, it became a hand-me-down for my younger brothers. But once I started going to school, even that benefit lost some of its luster.

You see, we were poor, so poor that the word should really have a few more syllables—pooooooooooor. All of our friends were poor, too, so we didn't notice it that much—until I started elementary school.

Today the old Trenton homestead, which is still in the family, has been cleaned up very nicely. Still, imagine two adults and nine children living there.
Photos courtesy of Elvin Bethea

At school, the biggest giveaway to my family's financial situation was my footwear. For most of my childhood, my parents put me in Brogans, an ugly work boot that was popular among us po' folks. I didn't like them, and I was too embarrassed to wear them to school. On the two-mile walk to school, I would stop about halfway, even in winter, and change into my sneakers, so that I wouldn't get razzed about my shoes. I was embarrassed by the size of my feet, too, because they drew attention to those dreaded Brogans. The kids taunted me about my feet with chants of "Tugboat" and then punctuated it with an impersonation of a foghorn. It hurt a lot, but I just ignored it.

I was never more aware of how much I didn't have than at Christmastime. (To this day my family calls me "The Grinch" because I still associate Christmas with poverty and deprivation.) We had to wait until Christmas Eve to buy our tree, because that was when the sellers marked down their product to get rid of them. It didn't take long to pick one out, because there was not much left. When we got the tree home, I went to the basement to fill half of a five-gallon bucket with coal for our tree stand. We usually threw some tinsel on the tree, and that was it. If we happened to get lights, only half of them ever worked, and it was a miracle the house never burned down.

Christmas breakfast was usually chitlins, which my mother cleaned the previous day to get rid of the smell, and hog maul (the stomach). Today, these are delicacies—you'd probably pay $18 a pound—but back then it was not considered anything special.

Every year I went to bed dreaming of finding the standard little boy fare, a BB gun or a slingshot, wrapped up for me under the tree—and every year I found a two-dollar shirt instead. The gift that came closest to fulfilling my wish was a hand-me-down sled from a friend of my mother's. One time in the late 1950s

Santa brought us a secondhand television set and a pair of pliers because that was the only way to change the channels.

It was Christmas dinner, though, that always brought a special treat that made me temporarily forget about the disenchantment of that morning. Every year my father got out his .22 rifle and herded the family downstairs. He told us to be totally quiet as he climbed upstairs to the second-story, where he could see the chicken coop from a window. "The Sniper" would then wait for the pheasants that liked to snag some feed from our chicken coop. As he had in his Army days as a marksman, my father took aim and got a perfect shot. We were not allowed to tell anybody about it though, because he didn't have a hunting license.

Mealtime was a whole different world in our household. We had to eat in shifts because the dining table only sat four. So all of the food would get placed on the table, and we'd reach in and grab what we could on our plates before moving into different parts of the house to sit down and eat. At dinner, that table was covered with dishes of collard greens, homemade biscuits with thick Caro syrup, butterfish (eaten bones and all), cornbread, pig's feet, pig's ears, black-eyed peas or pigeon peas, and crackling bread (boiled and dried hog skin baked into the cornbread). If my father wasn't given rice with every meal, there was going to be an argument. To this day I still won't eat cornbread, because I had so much of it as a child. We grew a lot of our own food in the garden, and my parents always made sure we were well fed. There were plenty of potatoes and onions, as I remember. I never went hungry.

One of the strangest food quirks in our house was my father's breakfast. We rarely had milk in the house, so he ate his morning corn flakes with water. Plain tap water. He never complained about it. He even tried to pretend that he preferred them that way.

My parents did their best with what they had. My mother had gone to college for a little bit, but my father only finished the sixth grade. They both worked numerous jobs to support our enormous family. My mother ran a beauty salon out of our home and cleaned homes for some of the wealthier white families in Trenton. Sometimes we even got small worn-out appliances given to us by the white women for whom my mother cleaned, and we found ways to make them work.

It was understood that as part of the family, the kids had to help out, and I learned a lot about hard work from watching my parents. One way I helped add to the income was by accompanying my mother in our old 1955 lime green station wagon as we picked up ratty old clothes and rags that people in Trenton didn't want anymore. (The driving around was half the adventure, because road salt had eaten away the floors of the station wagon. You could see the road beneath your feet as we drove, and placing a rubber mat over holes was only a temporary fix. In the winter, the slush from the melted snow and ice splashed right into the car.) We brought the rags back to our garage and bundled them up for the ragman. We took the bundles to a weigh station, and then we got paid based on the weight of the rags, almost like you would with cans or metal today.

For me perhaps the most unsavory job was the one that earned me the nickname, "The Chicken Man." One time when I was about 11 or 12, we went to Snow Hill, Maryland, the chicken capital of the world, to visit Uncle Henry, my mother's brother. Uncle Henry kept chickens on his farm, and the chickens fascinated my father enough that he got Uncle Henry to teach him how to raise them. When we got home, my father converted a previously unused 30-yard-by-40-yard building on our property into a chicken house. He set up a complete chicken farm with chicken wire fences and all of the trimmings.

My old nemesis, the chicken coop, has fallen on hard times. I don't miss it one bit. **Photo courtesy of Elvin Bethea**

At first my job was to water, feed, and tend to these horrible chickens. I hated it with a passion. Every time I entered that coop, there were two things to deal with—the smell and the chaos. It only got worse as I got older and my responsibilities widened. I then became their judge, jury, and executioner.

Every weekend it was my job to go out to the big apple trees near the chicken house and prepare the gallows and the cooking pot. I had created a makeshift chicken-catching device out of a coat hanger with a loop on the end, and I stuck the instrument into the coop, lassoed the skinny legs of a chicken, and dragged it out of its home. The bird squawked and flailed as I hung it over a tree branch. Then with a sharp knife, I caught the animal by the neck and cut its throat. Blood and feathers flew everywhere as I waited for it to bleed out. Then I placed it in the hot water—but not too hot, or the skin would come right off. I then plucked the bird and put it over another fire to singe the remaining small hairs. Then came the cutting and processing. I did this about 20 times for a good day's work. I won't even try to describe the smells. I wouldn't be able to do them justice. It was just part of life on the farm.

We had some economical methods for replenishing our supply of biddies: Instead of buying them, we always brought a few back from Uncle Henry's, but more often we made regular visits to the city dump. Yes, the city dump. Several chicken farms would decide that a batch of birds was just not worth having, and so they discarded them at the dump. I discovered one of the reasons I believe that these chickens were left at the dump—many of them were cannibals. I watched the chickens peck away at the weaker or injured birds until they died. I hated being "The Chicken Man" with a passion.

My father worked in the local junkyard, scrapping cars, and in construction, doing whatever jobs were available. He drifted from job site to job site, digging ditches, laying tile, putting up dry wall, etc. He also was a numbers runner for the local mob. Betting on numbers was a popular way to gamble in the 1940s and 1950s. People put money down on a certain combination of numbers, and the runner took their bets and held the cash until the winning set of numbers, usually generated by a formula involving numbers from the newspaper—stock closings, sports scores, etc. Some bettors even used dream books to pick their numbers. For example, if someone had a dream about a train running off a cliff in the rain, they'd look in the dream book and the train would be a three and the cliff would be a five and the rain would be a seven. Then they'd play the game by betting on 3, 5, and 7.

My father went around to bars and restaurants and picked up the bets and money. Then every Saturday, Vic, this Italian guy, came to the house and picked up the money.

As a 10-year-old kid, I became my father's accomplice in his numbers running. I remember going in the back doors of restaurants or even private homes to pick up brown paper bags of money. I was the perfect bag man, because no one suspected a kid, walking around these places with a paper bag. They would have thought it was my lunch or my marble collection. As I got older, and much bigger, it looked more suspicious, and because it *was* illegal, I was in greater danger of getting in trouble, so my father stopped using my services for this particular side job.

Later when I was a strapping teenager, I joined my father on several of his jobs. I worked construction and in the junkyard for a few years. We had the unenviable job of cutting out engines and various motor parts from junk cars. The wintertime was the worst. I bundled up as much as I could, but there was no escaping the cold. We kneeled down on a flattened cardboard box on the snow-covered ground and crawled around under some rusted-out junker searching for some obscure part for hours every day. It was when I was underneath those jalopies and spading shovelful after shovelful of dirt out of ditches that I realized how important it was that I go to college. I had to improve my way of life, and I never wanted have to work multiple jobs for minimum pay and struggle to feed and clothe my family.

Chapter 2

"THE BEAR" IS BORN

Thanks to the drudgery of the chores I did when I was growing up, I turned to sports in my adolescence to get a break from the hard work. I fully intended my time on the field to be an excuse for a lighter load at home, but that somehow never happened. My chores were always waiting for me when I got home after practice.

In sixth grade I started playing soccer—at fullback—and then baseball—at pitcher. I just loved both sports. As far as I was concerned, soccer and baseball were *it*. But unfortunately my athletic career was almost cut short during the last soccer game of my eighth grade year.

During the game, I moved in to trap the opposing team's forward, making it difficult for him to hook the ball around me and break for the goal. As we battled, the player drew back his leg and belted the ball into the air. Wham! It hit me in the eye point blank, and everything went black. I fell to the ground, covering my eye. "I lost my eye," I thought, and I was sure my eyeball was rolling around on the field somewhere.

I was rushed to the emergency room at Helen Fald Hospital in Trenton. The eye was totally swollen shut, and I was scared. My eye doctor in Trenton arranged for me to be admitted to Wills Hospital in Philadelphia where I had to lie in bed with my head tilted down at a 40-degree angle so all of the blood would rush to my head. If this primitive method didn't do the trick, I was going to need surgery. To me, though, the worst part about the hospital stay was the cold bedpan. (Do they chill those first?)

Ten days later my vision returned, and I slowly got better, but the doctor warned me that I was never to play any contact sport again—no jumping, no bouncing, no hitting, no nothing. Three weeks later I was able to go home, but after 21 days in bed, getting up and walking was no picnic because my equilibrium was off. The saving grace was that the accident happened in a school game, so the district paid all of my medical expenses. If it had been a pickup or sandlot game, my parents would never have had the money to give me that kind of medical care.

Despite the warnings, my friend Herb Flamer and I were determined to try out for the high school football team the following year. Mind you, we knew nothing about football (except that Flamer was always the kind of kid who knew about *everything,* regardless of whether he knew *anything* about the topic) but that didn't stop us. We were saved a lot of embarrassment before the football tryouts when our buddy Donnie Harmon came home for the summer. Harmon had spent his first year in college, and during that time he had fallen in love with football. He talked about nothing else.

Harmon took Flamer and me to the Lawrence Township Armory, where the armed forces practiced their maneuvers, and he showed us a three-point stance. He demonstrated, and we copied him. It seemed easy enough, and the contact sounded like it would be fun. My only concern was getting this past Mom, who knew, of course, about the doctor's advice to avoid contact sports.

Fueled by Harmon's enthusiasm and my own curiosity, I decided to just keep everything a secret from my mother. I snuck out and showed up at the Trenton High School field that Saturday afternoon, expecting to be rejected. To my surprise, I made the cut.

Keeping up my deception didn't seem as hard as I thought it would be, because I used to stop at Flamer's house after school every day to do homework. That helped explain my lateness from school after football practices. After the first few practices I came home with a few scrapes and bruises, but those were easily excused as adolescent rough housing. Everything went well until the local Trenton paper covered one of our practices, and my name got into the story. My mom happened to scan the page and see my name. It could have been a lot worse, I suppose. She wasn't thrilled, but she didn't really react too negatively, and as long as my chores were still getting done, my father was neutral about it. As far as my father was concerned, if you weren't working, then you weren't doing anything. Sports? His favorite sport was yard work.

Despite her initial lack of enthusiasm for the sport, my mother did eventually accept my decision to play football and even drove me to and from practice at odd hours in all kinds of weather. I don't have any recollection of her ever coming to a game, however. I know for a fact that my father never attended any of my games, because Saturday was a workday.

After a few more practices, Trenton Tornadoes coach Pat Clemens moved me up to the varsity squad where I played running back, offensive tackle, and defensive tackle. Coach Clemens was a short, gray-haired and seemingly ancient man, although he was probably only about 50 years old. He did football by the book. He was tough as nails, and he didn't hold anything back when we frustrated him or made him mad.

One time we had a big game against the local Catholic high school, Notre Dame, and I was on defense. The quarterback snapped the ball, and I ran forward to block my man. Right as I got to him, the running back blazed past us, and while still blocking, I turned and watched him move through the hole. The local paper happened to snap a photo right at that moment, and Coach Clemens seized it to make a point. The next day he posted that picture of my big no-no on the wall of our locker room, turned to the entire team, and lectured, "This is the way you *don't* block!"

At the time I was operating on pure instinct, because I really had no inkling what the game was all about and quite honestly didn't really even understand the rules. But I thrived under Coach Clemens's strong hand. We always knew when he was pissed off, because he'd start to mumble to himself and keep his

It's "The Bear"! My good buddy Tim Masick (No. 31) and I enjoyed our time as Tornadoes. **Photo courtesy of Elvin Bethea**

eyes on the ground. He'd yank you out of a game for one mistake and then leave you out for a good long while to let the lesson sink in. He'd also run the hell out of us in practices. We were treated to the old run and die. Coach had us doing sprints from sideline to sideline at the 50-yard line until we just wanted to die. Coach Clemens's perfectionism and toughness pounded me into the football player I was to become, and he wired me to prefer coaches who were taskmasters.

I had been known as "The Bear" by my neighborhood friends ever since I had a growth spurt at age 12. Junior Taylor, another poor kid who came from a family of 12 kids, gave me the nickname because of my size. I was always the biggest kid in our group. The nickname got picked up in high school when I began to get some recognition for playing football. Before too long, the whole town knew me as "The Bear."

Despite having a catchy nickname that was mentioned regularly in the sports pages, I was not the star of the high school football team. That honor went to my good friend Tim Masick, the Tornadoes' fullback. Masick was a real ladies' man and actually had groupies following him around! I was just a big, dumb lineman.

But on the track team, I was like a rock star. (I had added track to my long list of sports not long after I started football. I had shot put in the summer, football in the fall, discus in the winter, and baseball in the spring.) My ego was much bigger when it came to track than football. I just knew I was going to win at every meet in which we competed. I held some New Jersey state records for many years, and my Trenton city records in the shot put still stand today. Trenton High School supported my efforts in shot put and discus to the extent that they even built a brand new footboard and installed a new concrete slab for me.

My favorite part of track was the aspect of competing against myself and controlling my own destiny. I always trained a lot

Bethea in California
'Bear' Heads West After Noisy Sendoff

By JOE LOGUE

Elvin Bethea is in California, transported by a sleek jet that failed to drown out the countless well wishes that completely buried The Bear yesterday when officials and students gave him a royal sendoff in front of Trenton High School. If wishing will make it so, Trenton's favorite son will make it big in the fifth annual Monterey Junior Chamber of Commerce Golden West Invitational Track Meet.

Given Plaudits

Cheered by students who had contributed to the fund that made his trip possible, Bethea, nattily attired, accepted the plaudits of Principal Vincent Halbert, Fund Drive Chairmen Walt Krichling, Carl Palumbo and Sheldon Ehringer, plus numerous other friends, then stepped into a Cadillac, supplied

and driven by Ulysses Thomas, for the trip to Philadelphia's International Airport.

Accompanied by Bob Callahan, assistant Trenton High track coach, his mother, Mrs. Henrietta Bethea, and two other friends, Elvin made the quick trip to Philadelphia where he and Callahan boarded the plane. They arrived in Los Angeles yesterday afternoon, reporting to meet

Work Out on Coast

LOS ANGELES — "It was a long, but interesting trip," Bob Callahan commented as he and Elvin Bethea returned to Marks Hall around 6 p.m. (9 p.m. EDT) last night after a workout on Cromwell field, which is located on the campus of the University of Southern California. "Elvin looked good; he really should be at his best for this meet."

Callahan is being quartered with another track coach in Marks Hall, within shouting distance of Bethea, and the two were headed for dinner after the workout and then a brief look at the sights. "We plan a hard workout Friday morning," Callahan reported. He also noted that the program from last year's meet lists the longest shot put at 65 feet, 7½ inches, a mark Bethea has bettered this year.

officials and ironing out preliminary details which normally accompany any athletic event.

While Bethea was airborne, the Elvin Bethea Fund also was in flight, the total amount figure rising with each passing hour. At the moment there is $2,266 in the fund, but that figure will not be the final one. A new, and higher, one will be recorded in the next 24 hours.

Big Ed Vereen, who as president of the National Negro Licensed Beverage Association, which also gave a sizeable donation, helped coordinate the drive, revealed yesterday that

his groups and individuals have contributed around $1,200 of the total amount. And Big Ed was still setting a fast pace when last seen yesterday.

List Contributors

Among his contributors yesterday were Dr. George Shepard Jr., Dr. Minor J. Sullivan 3rd, Edward L. McIntyre, Cicero Davis, Fred Vereen Jr., Jim Carlton, Leroy Green, Thomas East, Robert Brown, Carl Di-toni, Ulysses Thomas of A. & M. Applicance, No. Willow St., and the National Negro Licensed Beverage Association.

In addition, the co-chairmen listed the following donors: $25: Charles Connell and the Lawrence Twp. Committee; Leslie A. Hayling, D.D.S.; $10: Dr. and Mrs. A. J. Migliori, Trenton Branch NAACP; James Moonon; $5: Bill Faherty, James Hall, Carolyn Moore; $2: Friend; A.W.S. and C.W.S., Mrs. Pearl's two sons, Joe Calorio; $1: Lee McConahy, Charles Sprague, J. Sisti, Virginia and Bob Ryan.

The Trenton High Alumni Association made a sizeable con-

(Continued on Page 34)

beered by THS students, who wave goodby, The Bear, who graduated this week, raises a giant hand, the same one that ntrol his shot put in the west coast meet. In addition to the t, Bethea also will compete in the discus at Norwalk,

Sportsman John Sanchez, proprietor of John's Tavern, hands a jar containing over $50 in coins, donated by San-chez and his customers, to Bethea Fund Drive officials.

Even the local paper covered me as "The Bear." **Courtesy of The Trentonian**

better by myself, because I knew how far I wanted to go in a training session, and when I was training with someone else, I felt like they might hold me back or they might not want to take it as far I would. Training alone kept me focused—it was just me.

Everyone recognized me for track, more than football, so I was convinced that track was my ticket to a college scholarship.

It never even occurred to me that I might go to college on a football scholarship until my junior year of high school. One day two football scouts from Morris Brown College in Atlanta came to a Trenton High game to check out two of my senior teammates. A few weeks later, they were both offered full scholarships to play football there. The idea of getting a college education on the strength of my football skills didn't seem so crazy after that.

Once my senior year came around, I was eager to see where football could take me in terms of a college scholarship. Initially Villanova and Pitt sought me out, but they shied away after viewing my high school grades. (As far as school went, I was just an average student. My favorite subject was history. I loved learning about anything dealing with the world and the changes that it has undergone over the years. I was especially interested in black history, but because this was the early 1960s, I had to get most of that from oral histories or just reading on my own. It was certainly not part of the school curriculum.) Most of the black colleges ended up making firm offers—Virginia State, Morgan State, North Carolina College, North Carolina A&T State, and Maryland State.

I had some good reasons to lean toward Maryland State. My much-adored grandmother, an angel on earth, lived right near campus and I thought it would be fun to have her so close to me during my college years. But when I visited the campus and saw it was in the middle of the woods—there was nothing there—my enthusiasm waned immediately.

Then I went and checked out North Carolina College. They offered me a full scholarship—half-track *and* half-football—and $15 a month for living expenses, which seemed like $1,500 to me. When I got there and saw that the women there were so beautiful, that sealed the deal. I decided right then and there that this was the school for me. I made a verbal commitment. So the die was cast, and my decision was made. Or so I thought. I hadn't counted on my mother's persistence and influence.

One Saturday before what I thought would be my freshman year at North Carolina College, I came home from work and found a white station wagon, sitting in our driveway. I thought nothing of it until I walked in the door and met the car's owner—Mel Grooms of North Carolina A&T. I also met my suitcase, which my mother had packed for me, and before I knew what hit me, my suitcase and I were riding with Grooms back to A&T. My mother had decided on A&T for me, because Mel Grooms, who was the offensive backfield coach there, was a high school classmate of hers. My mother had spoken, so resistance was futile.

Once on campus, they stashed me in an empty dormitory room. There I was somewhere in the wilds of North Carolina— alone and held captive. A&T staff ushered me to the head coach's house for meals and snuck me around campus for a tour, but almost everything was done under the cover of darkness. I felt like a political prisoner.

One night I was alone in a room/cell at A&T when a surprise visitor knocked on my door. I opened it up, and there stood Norman Tate, a track athlete at North Carolina College who would go on to become a famous Olympic quarter-miler.

"We found out they had you here, and so they sent me to get you out of here," he whispered. "Come on."

We stole back to NCC under another cloak of secrecy. It was like living in a James Bond movie.

When we got to campus, Tate took me to the head football coach's house. The coach paraded a long list of perks I could have if I were to go one step further and make my commitment official, not just verbal.

"Look, all you have to do is show up," he said with his best salesman smile.

"That's great!" I exclaimed wide-eyed at the vision of all those gorgeous young co-eds at North Carolina College. "Just let me go back to the A&T dorm and get my things."

They never saw me again.

A&T kept a very tight leash on me thereafter. I knew that there was no point in even considering any other college now that my mother had chosen A&T for me. An 18-year-old kid thinks he's in heaven when these schools recruit him, because they trot out all of the prettiest women and make their campus irresistible to his raging hormones. I was no exception, but I was being pulled in several different directions. Virginia State had the prettiest women, North Carolina had Olympian Norman Tate and great track facilities, Maryland State had my grandmother nearby, but North Carolina A&T State had the trump card—my mother. I was destined to be an Aggie.

Chapter 3

"PLAY LIKE YOU PRACTICE, PRACTICE LIKE YOU PLAY"

In the fall of 1964 I headed to Greensboro, North Carolina, to enroll in North Carolina A&T State on a half-track, half football scholarship. It was a pretty good deal for A&T; they got two athletes for the price of one. Well, actually, it was less than the price of one, because A&T was a tiny poor black college.

But although A&T wasn't my first choice and wasn't a prestigious school, like Villanova or Pitt, I can't imagine going anywhere else. Sometimes I wonder what I missed out on, though.

Ultimately my A&T experience was made by Hornsby Howell. I first met Hornsby Howell when he wasn't even a coach. He was actually the team trainer. He taped me up, he rubbed on liniment, and he generally tended to our aches and pains. He seemed soft-spoken and genuinely kind. It was short-lived.

In my sophomore year, the quiet, gentle Hornsby Howell became Coach Howell when he was put in charge of the defensive line. Shortly after he became our coach, he brought us out onto the field to conduct his favorite training exercise called "The Bull in the Ring."

He had 20 of us count off numbers and encircle a single player. He waited as we all got into position.

"Now," he bellowed. "I am going to call out a number. The player with that number has to charge the guy in the center. You in the center are supposed to throw a block on the outside guy. Okay, Number 6!"

The No. 6 player barreled in at the lone defender. Smack! They clashed and battled it out.

"Number 1!"

Smack! Another block. The guy in the center faced off at the top of the circle, ready to counter

"Number ... 15!"

Smack! No. 15 sandblasted the guy from behind. He wasn't even ready.

Coach Howell smiled.

"You can either be good, or you can be gone!" he shouted at the player in center.

The crushed player nodded as he tried to shake away the stars. The drill continued, and Coach Howell waited for the player to commit and then called a number behind him. He seemed to enjoy watching his players get decked.

"This is a very sick man," I thought as I saw how much he enjoyed the pounding.

And that was only the beginning. The sweet, lovable, laid-back man who had so carefully wrapped my feet in the locker room now thirsted for violence on the field. I was amazed, and thrilled, to watch firsthand the transformation of Coach Howell from Dr. Jekyll to Mr. Hyde. He got so excited after every jaw-breaking, hard-hitting play in practice that he would jump up and down on the sidelines while grabbing his crotch. He was possessed.

His maniacal intensity was matched with a demanding perfection. He constantly belittled players to get them to work harder. His classic comment was "You're so damn sorry, I should have given your momma the scholarship and left your sorry ass at home." One time during practice a player kept making mistakes over and over again. Finally Coach Howell blew the whistle and brought practice to a stop.

"Go and get me some gasoline!" he ordered one of his assistants.

The assistant hurried off, and we all thought that Coach was kidding. But a few moments later the dutiful assistant came back with a gas can.

"Take off your goddamn uniform and put it in a pile over there!" he barked to the terrified player.

The player peeled off his jersey, pants, and pads and placed them right where Coach had pointed. He stood there shaking in his undershirt and jockstrap as Coach Howell grabbed the gas can and doused the articles.

"Who has a match?" he asked, and it was quickly provided. Coach lit the match and dropped it onto the soaked pile. "Goddamn it, *now* you can't contaminate the rest of my goddamn team! Get your sorry ass off the field!"

We watched in horror as our former teammate slinked off the field and the uniform smoldered and burned into ashes. We never saw that guy again.

Coach Howell believed in the philosophy "Play like you practice, and practice like you play," and he pounded it into our heads from day one. In practice every day we did all-out hitting. There was no saving strength for games. In fact it felt like all we did was nonstop hitting from the moment practice began until the second practice was over. That's probably an exaggeration, but it's still how it felt to us. He ran us through the woods behind the field house at 6 a.m. in pitch darkness. Then he'd have us roll down the hill and do bear crawls back to the top. On game days, we'd suit up in the field house, which was no bigger than my garage, and then walk down Louisiana Avenue for a full mile in full gear to the stadium, and unless you were knocked unconscious in the game, you had to walk back, too. Those were the days.

Coach Howell made me the player I became. He formed my work ethic and built the whole foundation for the way I thought the game should be played.

Our A&T teams during my time there were better than average but not spectacular. We were always above .500, but after winning our division in my freshman year, we never won anything else for the next few years. One of the biggest kicks I got during my college career was playing at four different positions in one game. It was a game against Florida A&M (where Bob Hayes would prove in every game that he really was the fastest man alive), and they destroyed us 60-0. By the time the game was finished, though, I had played offensive tackle, offensive guard, defensive end, and even linebacker. I may have even done some kicking in the game, but the heat and humidity were so horrible that day in Florida that it has affected my memory!

In our games against Tennessee A&I, I had to face the legendary Claude Humphrey (who should be in the Pro Football Hall of Fame) for the whole 60 minutes. We both played both sides of the ball, so I had to face him at defensive end *and* offensive tackle for the entire game. I don't recommend to anybody facing off with Claude Humphrey for 60 minutes! His completely dominant play on defense was a major contributing factor in Coach Howell's successful argument for me to reduce my time on the offensive line.

Even though I benefited from excellent coaching, A&T didn't have sufficient money to provide a lot of the basics that other universities offered. The athletic facilities were poor. For football, they couldn't afford to have lights on the practice field, so when we practiced after dark, which was often, we'd drive some cars around the field and turn on their headlights to shine some light on the action. They also never had the proper setup for the shot put and discus throw. They had a horrible cinder track that tore up your legs if you fell. During my recruitment the athletic department promised me, "We're going to have a new stadium here." Well, the new stadium and improved facilities never happened during my tenure at A&T, but I did get a new toe board for shot put and discus.

Our equipment always consisted of hand-me-downs from a white university, and we had no washers and dryers so our uniforms had to be sent out to the campus laundry *only once a week*. By the third day, your uniform stank so badly, it actually started speaking to you.

The school provided our meals, but if you missed lunch on Sunday, you didn't get to eat again until Monday morning. At Sunday lunch, we were given a doggy bag of greasy roast beef that was supposed get us through until breakfast the next day. After a few weeks some of us got our hands on a hot plate to share, and we crowded around it to fry up some bologna and cheese to tide us over. That bologna and cheese got us through a lot of lean times in college. (My parents always made sure I had a care package to take back to A&T after my visits home. They filled it with peanut butter, strawberry jam, sardines, and Vienna sausages.)

Travel was also economical. We either slept on the bus or stayed at the fleabag motels in the area that allowed blacks. But whenever we played at Maryland State, there were no hotels for blacks nearby, so we took the 13-hour bus ride up, and Maryland State allowed us to use the bunk beds in an abandoned train depot on campus for lodging. We slept until around 3 a.m. when a train passed through and blew the horn.

We were one of the few black colleges with a decent bus, so when we went on the road for track meets like the Penn Relays or the Florida A&M relays, we loaded up our 15 guys, picked up the track team at Johnson C. Smith College in Charlotte, and then met the Winston-Salem team halfway. There were never less than two schools on that bus.

The athletes had a motto when I was in college, "If you can make it at A&T, you can make it anywhere in the world."

But I couldn't really complain about the situation, because I was lucky to be there. I was an average student in high school and college, and I even had to repeat remedial English three times my freshman year at A&T. My best subject was kinesiology, and I wanted to be a masseur. My hands were certainly big enough for physical therapy, and that's what I really wanted to pursue after college. I've never regretted that I didn't go to a bigger, richer school.

My senior year, 1968, was an exciting time for a number of reasons. On the serious side it was a time of enormous social and political unrest. Greensboro and A&T had a history of being involved in the Civil Rights Movement. On February 1, 1960, four A&T freshmen had staged a sit-in at the local Woolworth's, protesting the fact that the store would not serve them at the "whites-only" lunch counter. This event launched sit-in movements around the country. A&T students continued to be involved in pushing for change, but in April 1968, a few days after Martin Luther King Jr. was assassinated, riots broke out in our small town. Some of the black rioters pulled a white truck driver out of his laundry van and beat him up. This brought the National Guard out, and as far as many of the rioters were concerned, a National Guardsman in North Carolina was nothing more than a Klansman in green fatigues. The guard rolled onto campus with M-50s attached to their jeeps, and they began shooting up one of the campus' oldest dormitories, Scott Hall. Those M-50 shells went through the brick building like a knife through butter. Scott Hall was finally torn down in 2004, but until then you could still see the bullet holes throughout the dorm.

But on a personal level, it was a time of looking to the future. For the second consecutive year I made the Black All-America team at three different positions: linebacker, offensive guard, and defensive end. I had noticed the NFL scouts, who came down to A&T all the time to check out players. In fact, during my sophomore and junior years, I had watched my teammates Cornell Gordon and Mel Phillips get drafted by the Jets and the 49ers, respectively.

While I was preparing for the winter track season, the AFL/NFL draft was conducted on January 30 and 31. Gil Brandt, the general manager of the Dallas Cowboys, told me the

Cowboys were going to pick me in the first round. I took him at his word and prepared to be drafted to Dallas.

The first round came and went. I wasn't a Cowboy yet.

The second round came and went, but I still wasn't a Cowboy yet, so I just forgot about it. Then one of the residents of my dorm came by my room.

"Hey, Elvin," he said. "The Houston Oilers are on the phone."

"What's a Houston Oiler?" I asked myself as I got up and walked down the hall to the phone. "Hello?"

"Is this Elvin Bethea?" the voice on the other end asked.

"Yes."

"You have been drafted by the Houston Oilers in the third round," the voice said.

"Well, um, there must be some mistake because Gil Brandt told me the Cowboys were going to pick me."

"I don't know about that, but the Oilers are going to offer you a contract to play offensive guard in the AFL."

Offensive guard? I thought I would be better on defense. Well, at least I knew now that the Houston Oilers were a professional football team.

I accepted a two-year contract with the Houston Oilers for $15,000 each year and a $15,000 signing bonus. It was a mind-blowing amount of money to me.

But overall it was a bittersweet experience. For track I had traveled all over the country and even to Toronto with legendary Olympian Bob Beamon as my travel partner. (Bob was a funny character and a typical New Yorker—he knew everything!) I loved wearing that suit with the AAU (Amateur Athletic Union) blazer when we went to track meets or the Penn Relays. When I wore that AAU patch, I felt like somebody. I had qualified in the shot put for the Summer Olympic trials in Mexico City, and I desperately wanted to go. I had looked at my competition at the

April 3, 1968

Mr. Elvin Bethea
236 Cooper Hall
Greensboro, North Carolina

Dear Elvin:

WELCOME TO THE HOUSTON OILERS.   We are delighted we
were successful in drafting you and look forward to having you
with us.

As you probably know, the Oilers will be playing all their home
games in the Astrodome this season and we know this will be an
exciting year.

Enclosed is a very beautiful and informative brochure on the
Astrodome which I think will be of great interest to you.

Kindest personal regards.

                              Sincerely,

                              Don Klosterman
                              Executive Vice President
                              General Manager

DK:df

Enclosure

The American Football League:
HOUSTON OILERS · BOSTON PATRIOTS · BUFFALO BILLS · KANSAS CITY CHIEFS · DENVER BRONCOS · OAKLAND RAIDERS · NEW YORK JETS
SAN DIEGO CHARGERS · MIAMI DOLPHINS

This letter from Don Klosterman made it official. I was a professional football player! Two interesting things about this letter: It mentions that 1968 is the first time the Oilers will play in the Astrodome and it was written the day before Dr. Martin Luther King's assassination. **Courtesy of Elvin Bethea**

trials, and I just *knew* I would make the Olympic team. Football was really secondary to all this, as far as I was concerned.

But it was either the 1968 Olympics or a career in football. I couldn't afford the luxury of the Olympics. I really only had one option.

When I received my bonus money from the Oilers, I gave half of it to my mother, and my parents bought a new station wagon.

I used the other half of the bonus for the down payment on a three-bedroom house with a nice lot in Greensboro. The house cost $15,000, and my monthly mortgage payment was $150. I was very nervous about how I'd ever be able to pay that banknote every month, but owning that house during the final months of my senior year at A&T was incredible. Because of my good fortune, my A&T football buddies and I ate for days. No more bologna and cheese on a hot plate for us! We had lived on those things for four years, but now it was Boss's Restaurant in Greensboro every night.

I immediately became the "Big Man on Campus." It was a short-lived status, though, because in a few short months I was demoted to AFL rookie.

Chapter 4

THE EDUCATION OF ELVIN BETHEA

Head coach Wally Lemm was a frequent flyer on the Oiler Express. He earned a spot on ESPN's list of Greatest Replacement Coaches for his remarkable achievement with the team in 1961 when he took over the reins in Houston after about three games and proceeded to take them on a 9-0 undefeated run that catapulted the Oilers to the AFL Championship. He then coached the St. Louis Cardinals in the NFL from 1962 to 1965 before owner Bud Adams brought him back to Houston in 1966. A lackluster year in 1966 (finishing 3-11) was followed in 1967 with the AFL East Championship and an impressive 9-4 record. So I had every reason to expect big things in 1968 when I arrived in Houston to entrust my football fortunes in the capable hands of Coach Lemm.

I first met Oiler owner Bud Adams when I came to Houston to sign my first pro contract. It was my first time in the office of a real businessman and, in Adams's case, a multimillionaire. It was filled with plush couches, and the walls were adorned with Native-American folk art. There was even a cigar store Indian in one of the corners. Adams himself looked like a big, rich, white guy. He was very cordial to me. Under my agent's advice, I signed on the dotted line for my two-year contract with a $15,000 salary and $15,000 bonus. I was 22 years old and fresh from a poor black college. I never expected to be playing professional football, but those astronomical salary numbers made it seem very real and incredibly serious. I had my contract, and now I had my chance to play pro ball.

My experiences at North Carolina A&T State did not fully prepare me for the revelations that awaited me in the AFL. I was an innocent, a veritable babe in the woods. I had a lot to learn about so many things, and the lessons flew at me fast and furiously.

The so-called agent who was helping me with my contract had promised to help me with some investments and was going

This is the obligatory contract signing photo op. Bud Adams Jr. is smiling because he got a bargain at $15,000 for each of my two seasons. I'm smiling because $15,000 is more money than my parents made in five years. **Lou Witt/Titans**

to guide me in directions that would maximize my contract potential. He wanted his 10 percent in advance, which amounted to $3,000, and there was just no way I was going to do that. Shortly after I arrived in Houston, I found out that one of my college coaches, Mel Grooms, had gotten a kickback in order to convince me to sign with this agent. Grooms had set up the whole thing, and he was paid by the agent who was now asking me for his commission in advance. I refused to pay the agent the $3,000 because he had hoodwinked me. The agent took me to court for the money.

Adams let me use his attorney to fight it, and on the day of the hearing, the so-called agent never showed up. I got to keep the $3,000, which was a great deal of money to me—it was roughly a year's salary for my father. However, the IRS audited me, and the whole agent debacle followed me around for three or four years. After that experience, I never used another agent during my contract negotiations. I took care of everything myself. Lesson learned.

On top of learning to finagle the art of contract negotiations, I was introduced to the politics of pro football during the first day of training camp at the Schriner Institute, a prep school in Kerrville, Texas. Camp had been delayed because of a battle between the owners and the players' union that had resulted in a lockout. The issues had been temporarily settled, and so the players filed off of the bus toward the dorms to get settled for training camp.

"Coach wants you to go straight out to the field!" an assistant bellowed as we set our stuff down. "No delays. No questions. Just move!"

On the practice field stood Wally Lemm, my first professional football head coach. I had never met the man, but that day he made sure I would never forget him. This little man was steaming, fuming, and was even hotter than the thermometer on that sweltering Texas afternoon, and he had a few choice words to say to the players.

"I don't like your union, and I don't like what they did," he said frankly. "They're not doing you any favors by keeping you out of camp, because it will be that much worse for you when you finally get here!"

Then Coach Lemm moved onto a blunt warning about complacency.

"Not everybody who is here today will still be here next week. The same goes for every week after that during the entire camp. We've only got 40 spots to fill, and the rest of you are just out of luck.

"Now get dressed and get back on this field! We are going to have a full three-hour practice!"

It was high noon in Kerrville, Texas, and hot as hell, but we didn't dare defy him.

Later that day I dragged my bags up to my room and met my new roommate, Lionel Taylor, a veteran player whom I had never heard of. Taylor was one of the best receivers in AFL history. He was at the end of the line in 1968, but he was filled with wisdom, and he took me under his wing. From the moment he met me, I was "The Rook" or "Rookie." We called him "The Old Goat." He was hard on me, but I appreciated it. Taylor was always laughing, and even more memorably, he played with a single bar across his helmet. It was really just there for looks, because he'd rather have played without a bar at all. If that wasn't enough, his pads were always paper-thin. Lionel Taylor had guts.

Coach Lemm was cut of the same cloth as Coach Howell. He was a taskmaster and a disciplinarian. He was tough on us, and he appreciated hard work. He didn't take any crap from anybody—sort of a Hank Stram without the colorful personality. Coach Lemm would cuss, but he did it so quietly that you couldn't hear it if you were outside of his immediate perimeter.

I arrived at the Houston Oilers without much of an idea as to what pro ball would be like. I quickly found out. **AP/WWP**

He did not suffer fools gladly and would not take no for an answer—especially from a player. He was my kind of coach.

Two of Lemm's assistants deserve some mention. F.A. Dry was the offensive line coach, and every time one of us screwed up, we'd hear his long, mournful drawl of "Son…." Whenever he called us "Son," we knew something was wrong. Bud McFadin was the defensive line coach, and I never gave him enough credit. He was a tough old cowboy who had played for the Oilers in the early 1960s. Coach McFadin had worked on oil rigs, he had a ranch, and he spit tobacco. He was one of the boys. He was like a white Coach Howell, and I appreciated his toughness and bluntness. Coach Dry wanted me on the offensive line, and Coach McFadin wanted me on the defensive line. It was nice to be wanted!

I came to training camp as an offensive lineman, but I also rotated in at defensive end whenever I was needed. The Oilers got a good deal—I played half of the practice in a red jersey for the offense and the other half in a white jersey for the defense. When preseason got underway, I was used exclusively on the offensive line.

During one of the preseason games, Glen Ray Hines went down with an injury, and I was called upon to line up against the Saints' fearsome defensive end, Doug Atkins. Atkins was six foot nine, about 290 pounds, and winding down a legendary Hall of Fame career, primarily with George Halas's Chicago Bears teams of the 1950s and 1960s. His trademark move was an effortless leap over offensive linemen that got him into the backfield and left a lot a bruised egos sprawled on the field.

Before I went in for Hines, Coach Dry advised me to try to cut Atkins off and keep him outside. Back then, an offensive lineman was not allowed to extend his arms away from the body. He had to block with the knuckles of his fists touching each other at his chest, with the elbows out at the sides. In my first few plays against Atkins, I was able to block him face to face. Then the next play I moved forward to deny him again, but he jumped skyward and did a leap frog right over me. You can be told about something like that, but until you see it or experience it for yourself, it's hard to imagine.

I turned to grab him and hustled him down, but every play thereafter he tried to go airborne, and I felt the frustration building inside me. The next time I held onto him to slow him down.

"Watch it, nigger," he said, almost matter-of-factly.

I had gotten to him. Atkins hated anything that slowed down his manic pursuit of the ball.

I glared at him from behind my facemask and stared him down.

"It's time to get serious about this job," I told myself.

I waited for the quarterback to hike the ball, and I couldn't wait for this mountain of a man to come at me again. I was pissed off, and I was determined to show Doug Atkins I could play in his league.

That was my welcome to the world of hardcore smashmouth football. Smashmouth is just good, old-fashioned, "old-school" football, the way the game was meant to be played. It's lower-your-shoulder-and-pound-them-in-the-ground football. Every game I wanted to chew the opponent up and spit him out and always let him know I had been there. Ideally, I made them think twice about taking me on so that my job became a little easier. Some people misinterpret *smashmouth* as being dirty football, because it is a particularly bruising style of play. It's not dirty, but it is punishing. The other guys were coming to punish me, so I punished them right back or better yet, punished them first.

But no matter how smashmouth things got during the game, as soon as I heard the final gun, I was always the first one to hug and congratulate my opponents—win, lose, or draw. My favorite adversaries were always the ones who could take the punishment,

Bear quarterback Gary Huff is about to get a hands-on demonstration of smash-mouth football. **Lou Witt/Titans**

give some punishment, and then forget it all after the game was over.

The first game of the regular season in my rookie year was also the first game that the Houston Oilers played in the Astrodome. Coming from North Carolina A&T, where we had to walk a mile from the field house to the rickety old stadium, it was quite a step up to be playing in the Eighth Wonder of the World. It was a whole different world at the Dome. I walked in there for the first time, and my mouth just fell open. No one else is pro football had a domed stadium, with air-conditioning and a carpet to play on, but we did. Everything in there was brand new and state of the art. Even the tape dispensers were impressive!

"This is where I belong," I remember thinking. "I could get used to this."

But this beauty had its disadvantages, too. There was a lot of turf toe among the Oiler players, thanks to it. The Detroit Lions lost three quarterbacks in one game on our turf. After years of use, the carpet just got so mashed down that it couldn't have been more than an inch thick. It was pulled so tightly over the metal rollers that it would actually shine. The shoes to wear when playing on Astroturf were closer to bowling shoes than football cleats. If you were making a cutting move on the turf and your foot caught, then your knee grabbed, and you had a serious injury on your hands. I once watched the crew put the turf down, and one of them told me that the Dome had the longest zipper in the world. There was a 10-inch-wide I-beam right down the center of the field and the two pieces of turf just got zipped up at the point where they converged. Somehow, zippers and football fields don't seem to be a natural fit to me.

One of my most vivid memories of the Dome is the animation on our Diamond Vision screen, which featured a raging longhorn with steam blasting from his nose that came charging across the scoreboard every time the Oilers scored. He'd kick up quite a fuss, and it made for a real show. Unfortunately, during our lean and hungry back-to-back 1-13 seasons, that cow took a lot of naps.

After the preseason game against the Saints, a story went around the league that Atkins had beaten me so badly I was switched to defense, but that's not really what happened. It wasn't until the eighth game of the season when we played Buffalo at War Memorial Stadium that the coaching staff made the move.

We were playing the Bills in late October, and the Oilers were doing well against Jack Kemp and his boys, despite the conditions of the field, which wasn't much better than the field I had played on in college. War Memorial Stadium was aptly named, because someone definitely must have held a war in there. It was a dilapidated disaster. It was nicknamed "The Old Rock Pile," but I called it "The Sand Pit," because there was a nasty pit of sand right in the middle of the field.

Buffalo's less than ideal stadium conditions were not confined to the field. The locker rooms were like something out of a Turkish prison. We were treated to freezing cold showers, and there were nails on the walls for us to hang our clothes on. The walls were so old and thin, that if you were quiet enough, it was possible to hear every word being said in the other locker room.

There also was a very narrow alley that the players walked to get to the field, and it seemed to take us right through the throng of angry fans in the stands. Oddly enough, there was something primitive about the stadium that made me think it was heaven.

I was standing on the sideline taking in the game and watching our defense during a Bills drive when Coach McFadin came over to me.

"Bethea, get in there," he muttered.

I wasn't sure I heard him correctly.

"But, Coach," I said, "the defense is on the field."

McFadin was blunt with me.

"I know who's on the fucking field! Now get your ass in there!"

He didn't have to tell me again. I ran onto the field and tapped Gary Cutsinger, our defensive end, on the shoulder. Cutsinger turned around, saw me, and his eyes widened. I was the last person he expected to see, and to say he was shocked would be an understatement.

I have to be honest and admit that I don't really remember much about the rest of the game, but years later I was told by Billy Shaw (the Bills' Hall of Fame offensive guard) that I made quite an impression. After a particularly grueling play, Stew Barber, the Bills' offensive tackle, returned to the huddle and looked at his fellow lineman.

"I don't know who this rookie is," he exclaimed shaking his head in amazement, "but he came to play."

Yes, I did. I came to play.

We beat the Bills 30-7, and I never played another down at any other position after that day. For the next 201 games of my career, I was a defensive end.

The high point of the 1968 season was probably the fact that it was the very first season that the Houston Oilers played in the Astrodome. Otherwise, we had a nondescript 7-7 season, which was good enough for second place in the Eastern Division of the AFL.

My rookie year also introduced me to two great players who became lifelong friends. Our brilliant outside linebacker, Garland Boyette, was a fantastic leader on the defensive side of the ball. Coach Lemm had been his head coach with the St. Louis Cardinals in the early 1960s, and Coach Lemm remembered Boyette, who was playing in the Canadian Football League at the time, when Coach Lemm came back to coach Houston.

Boyette was a smart linebacker who really knew the game and was a whiz at stopping the run and plugging holes. In my new position on defense I was able to learn from him. When I came to the pros, I was a bit of a renegade who got a little reckless on the field from time to time. Because I could get off of the snap quickly, I wanted to take a gamble and try to make a big play. Boyette kept me in line.

"Cover the hole first and keep those offensive linemen off of me!" Boyette yelled at me invariably at some point in the game during my first season.

"Hey, I want to get a piece of the action, too," I smarted back.

Eventually, we found a system that worked for the benefit of the defense as a whole, and we each still got to have some fun hunting down the ball carrier. Boyette was a philosopher of defense, and it was like having another coach on the field for me. He kept me in line on the field and helped me channel that tendency toward taking risks into a more successful strategy at my position.

Boyette was a great teammate and is still a lifelong friend.

Kenny Houston was only in his second year in the league but was already establishing his dominance in the secondary and his role as a great leader on the field. Kenny was incredibly vocal and generous with his support of his defensive teammates in the heat of battle. We could all hear him back there in the secondary over the snap count and the crowd noise, and it got all of us on the defensive line charged up and ready for action. We all believed in him and got behind him as a leader on our defense. Everyone could tell, even then, that he was destined for the Hall of Fame.

Kenny was one of the smartest football players I ever saw. He knew exactly where to be and when to be there. He also was a hard worker. We called him "The Preacher," because he was an inspiration to all of us and everyone went to him for a little moral uplifting.

He was a rare breed of a man. On the field, he was 200 pounds of fierce and ferocious punishment for wide receivers, but off of it, well, he was different. One time during training camp, Kenny and I were bored in Kerrville, which is not a surprise given that Kerrville is smack dab in the middle of nowhere. The opportunities for entertainment in Kerrville ranged from slim to none.

In the late 1960s, there was very little for the black guys to do and few places we were even allowed to go. The options were hanging out at the Dashiki Club, fishing, or sleeping. That's about it. Usually it was always so hot after practice that there wasn't much you wanted to do anyway.

That year we had the use of a Jeep, and Kenny had brought along his .22 rifle, so we went out to explore the wilds outside of Kerrville. We decided to go shoot some jackrabbits.

Well, I had never shot a jackrabbit in my life, and I'm pretty sure Kenny hadn't either. I didn't really even know what we would do with one if we happened to bag it. Where I grew up, we shot Christmas dinner but not little jackrabbits.

Before I could solve this predicament, we ran across some jackrabbits and Kenny zeroed in and took a shot. He nailed a rabbit, and it jerked, let out this high-pitched squeal that pierced the quiet wilderness around us, flopped around a little, and then died. We gave the jackrabbit a proper Christian burial, and Kenny probably gave a little eulogy.

On the drive back to camp, Kenny was unusually quiet. He was always joking and laughing, but his normally cheerful face was racked with sadness in that Jeep.

"What's wrong, Kenny?" I asked him.

"It would've been okay, Elvin," Kenny said softly, "if he hadn't squealed."

Players don't come any better than Kenny. He was fast, quick, agile, smart, and a brutal tackler. People don't come any better than Kenny, either. He is warm-hearted, generous, loyal, and deeply religious, with a heart as big as Texas.

At the end of my rookie season, I had learned a lot of the art of football, the AFL, and life. Segregation and racism were not new concepts to me when I arrived in Houston. It existed to a relatively small degree in Trenton and then to a much greater degree during my college career in North Carolina, but now I was in Texas. Geographically, I was moving progressively more backward in the areas of race relations.

One of the ways this was most evident was on the team bus. Although it was never legislated by the team, the white guys gravitated to one bus and the black guys got on the other. The players somehow had this racial division stuck in their heads even though no one was stipulating that this was how it had to be. I think it was really subconscious on their part.

Sometimes I wandered onto the "white" bus for the ride back to the airport after a game. I climbed up with my gear and sat down in a seat.

As I boarded the bus, I got shocked looks from some of my white teammates and some good-natured ribbing.

"What are you doing here? You're on the wrong bus!"

I usually gave it right back to them.

"What do you mean 'wrong bus'? We all play for the Oilers, don't we?"

It never got too ugly, and I never let it really bother me. All I wanted to do was play ball, make a small paycheck, and go home when the game was over. The sacrifices made by athletes like Jackie Robinson, Willie Mays, or Jim Brown were almost impossible to fathom, compared to the comparatively small inconveniences that black players faced in the late 1960s. These feelings ran deep in some players' minds, though.

After my rookie season in 1968, I headed back to Greensboro, North Carolina, and tried to get an offseason job. There weren't many jobs to be had, except for some factory work in the tobacco plant. After a year as a professional football player and four years of college, that seemed like a big step backward. So I took a few classes that I needed to finish my degree and received my bachelor of science in physical education right before I headed to camp for the 1969 season.

The 1969 season would have been uneventful for the Oilers (we stayed at .500 with a 6-6-2 record and achieved another second place in the East) except for the fact that we made the playoffs. We played the AFC Divisional Playoff against the Oakland Raiders on December 21, 1969. It was a great game—for the Raiders. Oakland scored four touchdowns in four minutes during the first quarter. We went to the locker room at halftime with a 28-0 deficit. Coach Lemm expressed his frustration with our uninspired performance by putting his fist through a chalkboard. It was 49-0 after the third quarter, and by the time we were put out of our misery, the Raiders shellacked us, 56-7.

With my first two seasons under my belt, I was much closer to some of teammates. As always, the Oilers never lacked for interesting personalities. Jerry LeVias had joined us in 1969. LeVias was a product of Southern Methodist University and made a big splash as the Southwest Conference's first black football star. He was certainly a bit on the cocky side, but he was also on the short side. He came into the league at five foot nine and 170 pounds, and when reporters asked him how he was going to deal with burly defensive players hunting him down, LeVias answered, "The bigger they are, the faster I'll run."

LeVias was a bachelor and earned quite a reputation as a ladies' man. In 1970, his second and final year with the Oilers, the big thing was bellbottoms. You had to have bellbottom pants to be a hit with ladies. We had just lost a game on the road to the

Patriots, and LeVias was late getting on the plane to return home. When he stepped onto the flight, he was decked out in his wide lapels and his bellbottoms. We would have called it a "sweet outfit." Coach Lemm was a stickler for punctuality to begin with, so it didn't help matters that we had just been shut out 24-0. The following week, Coach Lemm covered all of the points he needed to cover about the upcoming game and then he concluded with a final thought.

"And if any of you want to wear bellbottom pants, join the Navy!"

LeVias never wore bellbottoms again.

George Webster had joined the Oilers a year before I showed up on the scene. He was not built like the prototypical linebacker. He was six foot five and only 225 pounds. I've never seen speed and range like Webster had at linebacker. If he was on one side of the field, and the play developed on the other side, Webster was there before anyone else to make the play. He was the first person to give me a nickname in the pros. He called me "The Beast."

You always knew that Webster came to play. He was a master at drifting back into the secondary and performing the same function as one of these current nickelbacks today. Quarterbacks weren't used to seeing a linebacker playing that deep, so we were able to mess up a lot of plays by creating some confusion.

Webster was one of the bright spots on the Oilers' defense in my first two seasons on the team. He made All-Pro both years and set a standard for me that I strived to achieve. The Hall of Fame voters even put him on the All-Time AFL Team although he only played in the final three years of the league. That's the definition of an *impact player*.

The 1970 season was the last season for defensive tackle Willie Parker who was about eight feet wide and 380 pounds. That's only a *slight* exaggeration. Parker was never serious about anything. He looked like James Brown's brother. He had some crazy hair and always wore burgundy, orange, or green—sometimes all at the same time! Every year they would have to go to Arkansas to retrieve him for training camp. He just didn't care.

Funnily enough, Willie Parker could play. He had serious skills, even if he never took life too seriously. Years after he retired, I had heard that someone went to Arkansas and saw him sitting by a lake, fishing with a cane pole.

That's just what I'd expect.

The 1970 season brought one big change—the AFL and the NFL merged. The merger, according to some, meant that now it could never be proven which league was better. There had been four Super Bowls up to then, and each league had won two of them. There's no question that the AFL had the players to match up against the NFL on a regular basis. The list of players in the Pro Football Hall of Fame whose careers began (or ended) in the American Football League is pretty impressive: Lance Alworth, Bobby Bell, Fred Biletnikoff, George Blanda, Willie Brown, Buck Buchanan, Nick Buoniconti, Larry Csonka, Len Dawson, Bob Griese, Kenny Houston, Charlie Joiner, Willie Lanier, Larry Little, Don Maynard, Ron Mix, Joe Namath, Jim Otto, Billy Shaw, Art Shell, O.J. Simpson, Jan Stenerud, and Gene Upshaw. Then there are the Hall of Fame coaches and executives who made their mark in the AFL: Al Davis, Sid Gillman, Lamar Hunt, and Hank Stram. As long as I'm on a roll, there's a whole slew of great players that never made the Hall of Fame, but their AFL careers could match up to anyone's in the NFL: Dick Anderson, Houston Antwine, Fred Arbanas, Stew Barber, Emerson Boozer, Butch Byrd, Ed Budde, Billy Cannon, Gino Cappelletti, Curley Culp, Elbert Dubenion, Mike Garrett, Cookie Gilchrist, Pete Gogolak, Goose Gonsoulin, Larry Grantham, Dave Grayson, John Hadl, Abner Haynes, Sherrill Headrick, Charley Hennigan, Winston Hill, E.J. Holub, Bobby Hunt, Rich "Tombstone" Jackson, Jack Kemp, Daryle Lamonica,

Floyd Little, Paul Lowe, Ron McDole, Jim Nance, Art Powell, Johnny Robinson, George Saimes, Tom Sestak, Matt Snell, Mike Stratton, Walt Suggs, Walt Sweeney, Bob Talamini, Lionel Tayor, Otis Taylor, Jim Turner, Jim Tyrer, George Webster, Jerrel Wilson, and so many more. Names like these convince me that the AFL was every bit the equal of the NFL. It didn't really matter in the grand scheme of things, though, because now we had become all just one big, happy league.

The merger of the two leagues meant that we'd be playing in some hallowed NFL stadiums from now on. The history that filled venues such as Soldier Field in Chicago, Lambeau Field in Green Bay, and Veterans Stadium in Philadelphia was overwhelming at times. It was hard not to think about the fact that these venerable stadiums were once the home turf for men such as George Halas, Gale Sayers, Red Grange, Vince Lombardi, Don Hutson, Chuck Bednarik, and so on.

Municipal Stadium in Cleveland was another of those NFL fields that gave me a sense of history from the first time I played there on November 22, 1970. Even though the showers were freezing cold and we lost to the Browns by two touchdowns, I loved the ramp that rose out of the locker rooms and led us onto the field. Our cleats would clack on the cement as we ascended to the arena. Then we'd appear at the top of the ramp so dramatically, it was as though we were Roman gladiators in a scene from some epic movie. I really felt like somebody. I got that same feeling in every game at Municipal Stadium over the next 13 years. My juices really got flowing whenever we made that Hollywood entrance in Cleveland. Then when I reminded myself that I was about to play on the same field that Jim Brown called home, it gave me goose bumps.

The 1970 season was not as successful for the Houston Oilers, however. We limped to 3-10-1 and finished fourth in our division. By then Wally Lemm was finished, too.

Coach Lemm was just tired, I think. He'd had enough. He didn't wait to get fired after that dismal 1970 season, so he just retired from coaching pro football altogether. I actually enjoyed playing for Coach Lemm, because he reminded me of Coach Howell from A&T. He didn't push as hard as Coach Howell did, but Coach Lemm was serious about any order he gave, and you had better not consider when you were going to get around to it. Just move!

Chapter

SIDEWINDERS AND TOKYO TURN-AROUNDS

Chemically speaking, I was pure when I came into the AFL in 1968. I didn't smoke, I didn't do drugs, and I didn't really drink (except for a little Everclear or Thunderbird on Saturday nights). It was all the rage in college to put peanuts in the bottom of your Coca-Cola, and I wanted to do that so badly, but I never drank Coca-Cola, because one of my college coaches always said, "Don't drink Coke. It cuts your wind." When I got to the pros, it was as if someone lifted a sheet to reveal to me what the real sports world looked like. Drinking a Coke would be the least of the temptations thrown my way in the big leagues.

My pro career was less than a year old when I joined most of the league and started taking pep pills. I remember going through my pregame routine in the locker room. As usual I had arrived three hours early and took my time getting geared up to play the Saints at Tulane Stadium. I listened as other players cranked up their music of choice—everything from county and western to funk, from classic rock 'n' roll to jazz, from R&B to gospel. I got dressed and reflected on what we were about to do on the field. I reviewed in my mind all the things we learned from the game films and from our practices during the week. I got myself in the right frame of mind to knock some heads together—and then I read Psalm 27 from my mother's Bible.

The LORD is my light and my salvation—
whom shall I fear?
The LORD is the stronghold of my life—
of whom shall I be afraid?

When evil men advance against me
to devour my flesh,
when my enemies and my foes attack me,
they will stumble and fall.

Though an army besieges me,
my heart will not fear;
though war breaks out against me,
even then will I be confident.

It was a superstition for me. Before every game I had to read those words. The Bible itself was not very imposing—it was black and about the size of pack of cigarettes. Those words gave me incredible strength, though. I felt I could take on anybody after reading that verse. It made me ready for battle. If I didn't read Psalm 27 from my mother's Bible before a game, I would have felt unprotected. I was not even going to tempt fate by testing what would happen if I didn't read it. (Once before a home game, I had forgotten to bring my Bible. I was frantic. I gave one of the locker room assistants my apartment keys and begged him to get it for me so I could complete my pregame ritual. It's a good thing we weren't on the road!) I played in more than 200 games during my NFL career, and I was nervous before every one of them—even the last one.

After I had finished my devotion, I was ready to play. I looked around the locker room and saw that everyone else seemed ready, too. Everyone was finishing up their routines and was dressed and was ready to play. I saw one guy grab a bottle from his bag and empty five or six pills into his hand. He downed them with a bit of water and continued preparing. Then another guy popped a few of his own as he finished dressing. Then another and another.

I wondered what they were doing, so I walked up to one of them.

"Hey, what are you taking?"

"They're pep pills, man," he replied nonchalantly.

"What do they do?"

"They make you feel great, so you can play better. Everyone takes them."

"Really?"

"Yeah, rookie."

I thought about that as I headed back to my locker. During the game I watched the guys I had seen take the medication and they seemed to feel fine, so I decided to conduct a little research. I discovered that *pep pill* was a friendly term for an amphetamine—and it seemed like I was the only player in the league not taking them.

"Don't you want to feel like those guys?" the trainer asked when I talked with him. "The other teams do it, too. You want to be competitive. You don't want to go out there naked. Come on and just take your medicine."

I didn't like to think that anybody had an edge on me when we got on the field. I thought about how the other players had said it helped them.

It didn't take much convincing before I was ready to join in the club.

The first time I took one of the pep pills, it relaxed me. I was so relaxed I could have heard a rat pissing on a cotton ball. Relaxed, though, in the sense that I was focused. As the game wore on, the pills made me feel more and more rambunctious.

I was still scared of a Coca-Cola, but now I was taking amphetamines—I mean, pep pills.

Well, I played so hard on every down that after I started taking the pills I had great difficulty in keeping my weight up and it was next to impossible to maintain a good weight. For the two years I took my "medicine," my weight fluctuated; I went from 250 pounds down to 238 pounds. That finally convinced me to stop taking them. I didn't want to get too small to be able to do my job effectively on the field.

They were also compounding my tendency toward air sickness on the return flights from road games.

The proverbial shit hit the fan for the Oilers, and the rest of the league, when the NFL cracked down on drug use in 1970. It became especially imperative for the league to take action after one of the Chargers' running backs played two quarters of football with a broken hip. The guy hadn't even realized he had been hurt because of the drugs he had been given. When the new drug guidelines came down from the league office, it was mandated that every drug administered to a player had to be prescribed and approved. Any illegal or unsanctioned drugs were to be immediately destroyed.

Bobby Gunn was our head trainer at the time, and he played it by the book. When the NFL drug inspectors came to the Oiler locker room, they found some unsanctioned drugs in the medicine closet. They ordered the drugs destroyed and warned the team that regular checks would be forthcoming. Gunn threw them all away.

But we had an assistant trainer nicknamed "Floogie," who had other plans and gave the players any drug they wanted. He wore a heavy winter parka, regardless of the heat and humidity, and always seemed to be fiddling and twitching like he was taking some of the pills himself.

Eventually the team released "Floogie," but before he took off for points unknown, he left a lot of the pills with two of his favorite players. One of these guys took all of the pills and poured them into a huge fruit jar and then buried it in his backyard. Well, the rains came, the heat and humidity added to the mix, and when the jar was finally excavated, the entire contents had melted together into a rainbow-colored block of illegal drugs. This colorful hunk of banished pills had every kind of drug imaginable in it. There were uppers and downers. There were *sidewinders,* which got their name because after taking one you never knew which side you'd wind up on. There were *Tokyo Turn-Arounds,* which would take you halfway to Tokyo before you had to come back for another one to get the rest of the way! These crazy bastards dried the pills, cracked the jar open, and broke off rocks of this solid mass of multicolored candy every time they needed a fix.

Later in the season we went to Cincinnati for a game. As everyone was in the middle of getting ready, the regular users on the team started to make their rounds of the locker room.

"You got anything?" they chanted from various areas of the room as they went from player to player. "You have anything?"

This time, they were out of luck. Out of desperation, somebody got the bright idea to chip off some pieces of this block of pills and take them before the game. Ron Pritchard, one of our crazy linebackers, broke off a piece for himself. I guess he figured he'd be fine because everything in the concoction was good on its own.

In the middle of the first quarter, Pritchard started shaking, twitching, and breathing erratically. We just thought he was hyperventilating.

At the half, when the trainers realized what he had done, they submerged Pritchard in ice water to bring him back down to earth. Pritchard almost died on the field that day, but any innocence I may have had left about what goes on in the NFL was definitely dead and buried.

Chapter 6

DWELLING IN THE AFC BASEMENT

n 1971 the Houston Oilers had a new man at the helm, Ed Hughes, and his style was a 180-degree turnaround from the powerful, forceful, tyrannical discipline that Coach Lemm handed down. Coach Lemm had motivated us through fear and strength; Coach Hughes didn't. He was quiet, too quiet. He was so quiet that he was completely ineffective at motivating players. Coach Hughes was a relaxed, easy-going, almost catatonic nonentity who was doomed to fail. Coach Hughes had no passion or fire at all. Mild-mannered and passive is no way to run a football team.

Coach Hughes's other problem was that he was saddled with a staff of assistant coaches who stabbed him in the back. His assistants were obviously doing him no favors in their approach to their coaching assignments. They wanted him to fail, so if Coach wanted to take things one way, his assistants took it another way. They would run plays without telling Coach Hughes and make him look bad. After an abysmal start of 1-9-1, it gets to be every man for himself on the team. None of the players wanted to feel like they were part of the problem, so we all tried hard to spare ourselves any embarrassment. I played full out *all* of the time.

Dante (Dan) Pastorini came to the Oilers in the 1971 draft. He was a good-looking kid from California who had tremendous athletic skills and was seen as the Oilers' "Great White Hope." He was going to take us to the promised land. Dan came to Houston with a great attitude and a warm personality that everyone embraced immediately. I always wanted to be like him because he had all of the women in the world.

If Dante was around, either on the field or off, you just knew something exciting was going to happen. He's just a great, great guy. He's the best quarterback I ever played with, and if he had been playing for any number of other NFL teams, he'd really have put up some Hall of Fame numbers.

From day one, Dan was an open, generous, loving guy whom you wanted in your foxhole, and he inspired tremendous loyalty from his teammates. He was our leader, and we would have followed him into hell if he asked us. He would've given the shirt off his back for any one of us. Dante always drove the kind of car that would make a defensive lineman drool with envy. Whenever any of us asked him to let us give his new sports car a spin, he'd just toss us the keys and say, "Sure, take it." That's Dante.

He got so many perks as the quarterback of the team, but he always made sure the rest of the players got to enjoy some of them, too. For instance, Dan got a deal with Datsun for the new Z-28. He arranged for each player to have the free use of a brand new Z-28 for one year. Some of the guys drove their Z-28s pretty hard that year, but I returned mine just as clean and pristine as the day I picked it up. Dan himself could be rough on his cars, too. I remember a beautiful Pantera that he wrapped around a tree while racing back to training camp after curfew.

Dante was my first choice of all of my teammates to be in attendance at my Hall of Fame induction, and I was thrilled to have him there. Whenever he asks me to be somewhere for him or to help him with anything that he's doing, I always try to make it, because he's always been there for me.

Kenny Burrough, our speedy wide receiver, came along in 1971, too. Burrough used to say that he could outrun a deer. To me, he always seemed cocky and appeared to really enjoy looking at his own publicity, especially the photos. He often said he was the fastest receiver in the league, and at the time he was. He used to announce to the team, "I'm not going across the middle," but he didn't need to go across the middle once he mastered the 75-yard catch along the sidelines. Some of those connections between Burrough and Dante were just poetry in motion. Dan could throw the ball a mile, and Burrough could run fast enough to be there when it landed. All we needed was an offensive line that gave Burrough enough time to run there and Dante enough time to throw it.

Any opposing defense knew they had to prevent those long Pastorini–Burrough completions if they wanted to shut down the Oiler offensive attack. When Earl Campbell arrived in 1978, Burrough's deep threat was somewhat diminished. However, he still kept defensive backs honest, and no Oiler fan could ever forget the sight of Burrough's double zero sprinting down the sidelines for one of those magical receptions.

We started off the 1971 season with a 31-0 beating by the Browns in Cleveland, a 20-16 downing by the Chiefs, and a 13-13 tie with the Saints. We lost the next three games and then edged the Bengals at home 10-6 before losing the next four games by a margin of 134-78. That 1-9-1 start made Bud Adams lose confidence in Coach Hughes fairly early. We came on strong at season's end, though, beating Buffalo, Pittsburgh, and San Diego in our last three games. Those last three wins bought us a modicum of self-respect, but 4-9-1 was still embarrassing.

Coach Hughes was not a bad guy, just a bad coach.

After Coach Hughes was fired, Bud Adams hired Bill Peterson, whose stints at Florida State and Rice had been impressive enough to warrant a five-year contract for about a million bucks. I think John Breen, the Oilers' general manager at the time, must have sold Adams a bill of goods on this Peterson guy. After all, when you really think about it, just how many college coaches, with no pro experience, have ever made a great career in the NFL? I can only think of one—Hank Stram. Friends, I knew Hank Stram; I've played in a Pro Bowl for Hank Stram; I was inducted into the Hall of Fame with Hank Stram. Bill Peterson was no Hank Stram.

It's very tempting to let Coach Peterson's Oiler coaching record just speak for itself. After all, what more can be said after he went 1-18 over the course of what could laughingly be called his NFL coaching career? That says it all, really. We were toiling under what was probably the worst two-season stretch that any NFL team has ever had to endure. He was one of Adams's biggest hiring mistakes.

However, I can't leave it at that, because if nothing else, Coach Peterson gave us a few laughs. We laughed *at* him, not with him.

Coach Peterson offered no discipline, no motivation, no control, no rhyme, no reason—nothing. He couldn't remember anyone's name, and his basic game strategy consisted of walking up and down the sidelines, smoking a cigar, and looking serious. He always called me "Alvin," and I never corrected him.

He was also known for his verbal miscues, and so we were never able to take him seriously. One time when Coach Peterson got frustrated with our bad posture during the singing of the national anthem, he barked at us from the sidelines.

"Get serious!" he shouted. "Just stand on your helmet and put the sidelines under your arm!"

My favorite one was the time he felt that it would really help our pregame preparation to have a spiritual moment. So he asked for someone to recite "The Lord's Prayer" aloud. He waited, expecting a volunteer. No one would do it. So finally with great resignation and solemnity, Peterson took charge. He bowed his head and began to speak.

"Now I lay me down to sleep..."

It was hard to contain the laughter so as not to break the reverence of the moment.

In Coach Peterson's first season with the Oilers, we dropped the first two games of the season before Joe Namath and his Jets came to town.

Everyone expected another Oiler loss, and that Sunday it looked as though it could come to pass. Namath was throwing every ball to the upper deck. He was just killing us in the air and was completing passes left, right, and center all afternoon. The defense was on edge, and in the defensive huddle, defensive back Willie Alexander was steaming mad, and in typical fashion for him, he was vocal about it.

"You guys have got to do your job!" he shouted at the defensive linesmen. "Put some pressure on!"

"Just calm down, Willie. Relax," linebacker Garland Boyette said in an attempt to calm everyone, especially Alexander, down.

We broke the huddle and headed back to face more of Namath's aerial bombs. More passing plays came our way, and as Namath's passing stats went up, Alexander grew madder and madder until he was jumping out of his skin and annoying the hell out of every one of his teammates.

Finally, Boyette called a timeout and went to the sideline. Coach Peterson asked why we were burning one of our timeouts.

"I'll tell you why, Coach," said the normally unflappable Boyette, "If you don't get Willie Alexander off the field, I'll throw him off myself!"

Alexander's mouth was always going, and sometimes that got him in trouble. He was our "clubhouse lawyer" and affectionately nicknamed "The Professor." If anything intellectual was being discussed among the Oilers, it probably originated from Willie Alexander.

Alexander was a talented defensive back. He had enough skills to pull down 23 interceptions during his career. Considering he was regularly facing wide receivers such as Isaac Curtis, Charlie Joiner, Lynn Swann, John Stallworth, and others who were much faster than he was, he had to make a difference in the secondary with brains and guile. He used his intelligence to find all of the best angles and positions for making a play on the great receivers in the AFC.

To me, Willie condescended to people a little too much, but that was probably just a byproduct of his intelligence. After witnessing an incident where I felt Alexander went a little too far with his superior attitude, he and I had a misunderstanding in the locker room. It was just one punch, but it was a good one, and I think he knew how I felt afterward.

(Alexander and I are good friends now, and I'm certainly proud of all of the great work he's doing with local Houston charities, not to mention his successful consulting business.)

We managed to get Alexander calmed down in that game against the Jets and stop against Namath and his offensive machine. When time ran out, the Oilers had their first (and last) win—26-20—of the 1972 season.

The next week we got a crack at a monumental first. The Oilers played in their first-ever *Monday Night Football* game. To make the thrill even greater, we were playing it in the Astrodome against the Oakland Raiders. We came into that Monday night game with a 1-2 record, riding high after our win the week before. We left the Monday night game with a 34-0 spanking by the Raiders that spelled the beginning of a long, dark descent for us. At least our national embarrassment in that game gave Don Meredith a chance for one of his best ad-libs. The ABC cameras prowled the nearly empty stadium to find an especially disgruntled Oiler fan in the Dome stands. Just as the camera zoomed in on the poor sap, he flipped his middle finger in disgust. "Dandy Don" recovered quickly.

"That fan thinks the Oilers are No. 1!" he quipped.

Is it any wonder that ABC did not come back to Astrodome for *Monday Night Football* until several seasons later?

Unfortunately the surprise win against the Jets proved to be the high mark. After losing to the Raiders, we dropped two more against Pittsburgh and Cleveland before heading to Cincinnati to play the Bengals.

With a 1-5 record the team was starting to feel the hopelessness of the situation. As the losses mounted, the atmosphere of the team deteriorated. We were a ship lost at sea, and the Houston Oilers became like a bad road company production of *M*A*S*H* or even *Animal House.* Because no one on the team respected Coach Peterson, or even paid him much attention, the team morale and discipline were completely unraveling.

On the bus before we played the Bengals, I was thinking about all of these things when I turned and noticed offensive tackle Elbert Drungo playing with something in his massive hands. The six-foot-five, 280-pound man opened his huge paws to reveal some Silly Putty. He took the putty and rolled a piece of it between his fingers, creating a long thin strip. Then he took another piece, rolled it into a ball, and put the ball on the longer piece. I watched him, fascinated by how this huge man could be so thoroughly entertained by a child's toy.

"What are you doing, Elbert?" I finally asked as he tore off four smaller portions of the putty.

He rolled them between his big thumb and pointer finger.

"I am making stick people," he replied in his slow high-pitched Southern drawl as he stuck the four little rolls, two arms and two legs, onto the longer part. "I want my hands to stay limber for the game."

I turned back in my seat and smiled at the picture. Elbert Drungo, the textbook version of a gentle giant. Drungo was such a quiet soul, and I think that was why we got along so well—especially when we were roommates from 1972 to 1977 and even when I beat him up in practice just for the fun of it. We were very close, so close that it hurt me deeply when he was traded to Buffalo after the 1977 season. After that, I swore I wouldn't get that close to another player, because it just hurt too much when he left.

Even after Drungo retired the next year and became a deputy sheriff in Mississippi, I always thought of him on the bus, playing with Silly Putty, and couldn't help but smile.

There were moments like those in the midst of the season. Unfortunately, no matter what steps we took to keep ourselves ready for the game, we always fell short. The Bengals nailed us 30-7, and we plummeted to the bottom of the standings as we continued to be beaten week after week. We capped the season against Cincinnati again, and this time we got a 61-17 shellacking by the Bengals, led by a young Kenny Anderson at quarterback.

The trading frenzy began in the offseason. In desperation to jar the team into success, we got players such as Tody Smith (Bubba's brother), Al Cowlings (yes, the same Al Cowlings from O.J. Simpson's Ford Bronco chase), and John Matuszak (who was dead before age 40 due to a lifetime of drug abuse). Gee, how could we lose with talent like that?

Matuszak was the Oilers' top pick in 1973. He was six foot eight and about 300 pounds, and "Tooz" was massive and mean. Off the field he was also a genuinely scary nut case with a serious drug problem, and I steered clear of him because of it. Then as we got deeper into the season he began to wear necklaces with the kinds of symbols that made it very clear he was worshipping Satan. "Tooz" came to practice loaded and looking like he had been up all night. He was always making excuses for his lousy play. This guy was a perfect physical specimen, but he wasted his potential. He had the body to be an all-time great, but he couldn't play his way out of cellophane. I suppose the lowlight of Matuszak's brief tenure with the Oilers, though, had to be the time he was issued a summons on the sidelines during a game. Now, *that* was a first! (Whatever else I felt about him as a player or a person, I find it incredibly sad that he died so young [38] at a time when it appeared he was putting all, that craziness behind him.)

In one of the biggest disappointments of my professional life, we also lost Kenny Houston in exchange for five players from the Washington Redskins. How could the Oilers trade a player like Kenny Houston?!? This was a future Hall of Famer who went to the Pro Bowl each and every year. I wasn't just losing a great teammate when Kenny went to Washington, I was losing a great friend. We used to go fishing after practice all of the time. I heard about the trade like everyone else did—on the radio. I even heard through the grapevine that I was on the trading block for being the "clubhouse lawyer" on the team. Hmmmmm. It probably didn't help that reputation when I became the Oilers' union representative for the NFL Players Association when Kenny left the team.

Kenny went on to do great things for the Redskins, and his Hall of Fame credentials were probably secured for him thanks to a play that Redskin fans refer to as "The Tackle." It was Kenny's first year in Washington. On *Monday Night Football* against the Cowboys, the Redskins were ahead 14-7, but Dallas was crouching on the Redskins' goal line at the four-yard line with fourth and goal and only 20 seconds remaining. Dallas's Craig Morton threw a pass to Walt Garrison, who got as far as the one-yard line before Kenny met him with a punishing hit and wrapped his arms around Garrison. There was a mighty struggle. Garrison tried to wriggle himself to the end zone, but Kenny dug in his heels and spun Garrison to the ground on the one. It was over, the Redskins took over on downs and ran out the clock, and the NFL had a new defensive superstar named Kenny Houston.

None of those five guys that we got from the Redskins in the trade proved to be worth losing a player like Kenny. We traded a pound of caviar for five cans of Spam.

The 1973 season didn't look much better considering what we had gained and lost. But Coach Peterson remained optimistic. During training camp in 1973, Coach announced that he wanted the team to focus on one word, and one word only—*Super Bowl.* That malapropism defined the season for us.

We opened the 1973 season against the Giants in New York and were soundly defeated 34-14. The next week we faced off against the Bengals in Cincinnati, where we lost 24-10. We returned home to play the Steelers and the Rams, only to drop those two games as well. When the Broncos came to Houston the following week, another lackluster performance led to another trouncing. After an 0-5 start—I guess we all forgot to focus on that "one word"—Coach Peterson was fired and replaced by Sid Gillman. Bud Adams hired Gillman, a future Hall of Fame coach, in 1973 to be the Oilers' general manager, and "Trader Sid" immediately set out to make the Oilers a better team by making several deals that brought in talent the franchise could build on.

In terms of coaching style, Coach Gillman was close to being another Coach Howell, and, in many ways, I liked that. However, Coach Gillman had us practicing for three hours at a time, and those were long, dreary, dismal, mind-numbing practices. A 90-minute uninterrupted practice was too long to be productive, but three hours (!) was downright dangerous. Injuries became more likely, and fights became inevitable. Coach Gillman had us running, not walking, *everywhere.* It was like being on a chain gang. I had to respect Coach Gillman because he didn't fool around. He was tough, occasionally even cold, but I thought it was a refreshing change from Coach Peterson. Sid Gillman would fire your ass on the spot if he thought he could make the team better. He was a motivator and a stern disciplinarian, and he talked to a player like he was someone who could make a difference—until that player couldn't make a difference anymore, and then he just cut him or traded him.

Coach Gillman had us playing as a unit again. We felt like a team. He may have used scare tactics to get us playing as a unit again, but sometimes there's nothing better for morale than having a common enemy to hate. A lot of the guys on the Oilers hated Sid Gillman. I certainly didn't hate him, but those three-hour practices didn't make me love him.

But things did not get better immediately in terms of wins and losses. Although Coach Gillman made an immediate psychological difference, we continued to fall short on the field. We went on the road and dropped our next two games to the Browns and Bears. The next week we went to Baltimore to face the Colts.

The Baltimore game was hard fought and high scoring. It went back and forth for four quarters, but the good guys ultimately prevailed. We beat the Colts 31-27. After the win, the team was ecstatic. Coach Gillman sent one of the trainers out to get champagne as we celebrated in the locker room and got ready to leave. Once we were all on the airplane, Coach Gillman presented us with the bubbly and we toasted our victory on the flight back to Houston. We thought the Baltimore game was the big turning point in our season, so we were celebrating as though we had already won the Super Bowl.

However, we were never able to capitalize on the momentum from the win in Baltimore, and we continued to lose, closing out the season with another 1-13 record.

In spite of a rough season as a team, I had a very good year on the field. I set the Oilers' franchise record for sacks in a season with 16, a record that still stands today. I also was selected to my third Pro Bowl.

After the 1973 season, Coach Gillman made some moves as general manager that set the Oilers moving in the right direction. He had a great eye for talent and brought in some phenomenal pieces to complete the puzzle for the Oilers' eventual success. He brought in Billy "White Shoes" Johnson on special teams. Midway through the season he traded away Matuszak to the Kansas City and got Curley Culp. Role players such as Willie Alexander at defensive back and Ted Washington at linebacker were coming along nicely. The team was starting to gel.

(Not that Coach Gillman was flawless in assessing a player's potential during his Houston Oilers years. He was, after all, responsible for drafting and then cutting a wide receiver from Tulsa who ended up enjoying a fair amount of success in the NFL. His name is Steve Largent. You can see his bust at the Hall of Fame the next time you're in Canton, Ohio.)

Coach Gillman also brought in a new defensive coordinator before the 1974 season named Oail Andrew Phillips Jr., more commonly known as "Bum." When I first laid eyes on Bum, the picture did not compute. He had a cowboy hat and cowboy boots, and he did not look like any football coach I had ever seen. He came with a great reputation for brilliant defensive strategy, though, and he had Coach Gillman's full confidence.

Bum wasted very little time in making over the Oiler defense. Personally, he tried to change my stance from a left-handed lean to a right-handed position. I resisted the change and was probably too vocal about it to the local press. On the team front, Bum installed a new 3-4 formation for the defensive line. I hated it. The strongest component of my game was sacking, and this drastically cut down on my effectiveness to get to the quarterback. My style of play was quick and upfield. I exploited my agility, my quickness off the snap of the ball, and my speed. I never had to worry about anything on the inside before, and now I had to learn to play inside and outside. The odds of getting your ass kicked in the 3-4 defensive line formation were pretty good. If I had continued to play my career in the 4-3, there is no doubt in my mind that I would have racked up about 250 career sacks.

Bum Phillips is probably making a vital game-breaking coaching point here. Because I consider Bum to be the greatest coach I ever had in the pros, I probably should have been listening to what he was saying. **Lou Witt/Titans**

If the 3-4 is tough on a defensive end, it's murder on the nose tackle. Along came defensive tackle Curley Culp from Kansas City. Bum immediately installed Culp in the new 3-4 formation at nose tackle, a hybrid between a lineman and a linebacker, and Culp made an impact. His job was to line up across the center and to plug the middle during rushing plays but to be ready to support the pass rush on passing plays. It took two or three players to block him, so there were some gaping holes created for Gregg Bingham, Robert Brazile, and me to wreak some havoc. With Culp on the job, we won our seven remaining games of the season and the 3-4 defense—no matter what I thought about it—began to work for us. Bum later said, "Curley Culp made me look smart."

During practices, Culp would line up against our center, Carl Mauck, and just beat Mauck up something terrible. It was like Mauck wasn't even there. Whenever Culp wanted to demolish an opposing player, he did it. He just wouldn't take anything from anybody, and everybody feared him.

(I don't expect I'll get much argument in professional football circles when I proclaim that Curley Culp was the best nose tackle to ever play the game. Nose tackles don't really get many chances to sack the quarterback because as soon as they get one blocker off of them, there's another one. When they get that one off, there's still another. However, in 1975 Culp got 11.5 sacks, became an All-Pro, and won the NFL's Defensive Player of the Year award. It's really a shame that Curley Culp did not get the press he deserved, because he just dominated and controlled the middle of the field for our defense. Culp was *the* man, among a lot of men. Hall of Fame voters, are you listening?)

Coach Gillman won 1974 Coach of the Year in the AFC for getting us to 7-7 that season, but there was trouble in the front office. Coach Gillman had been serving as general manager and head coach, and Adams thought that Coach Gillman could not justify spending the kind of money he needed to spend to build the team, so Coach Gillman quit both jobs. He had been the first NFL coach to use a computer in order to input downs, distance, and play choice probability for opposing teams. He was always the first one at the stadium and the last one to leave. His coaching style rubbed a lot of players the wrong way, and when he left Houston, there was a party on every block. However, he was a no-nonsense guy, and I respected him.

After resigning from the Houston Oilers, Sid Gillman never coached again. He did, however, build a great foundation for a winning Oiler team that carried us through the late 1970s and got us out of the AFC basement.

Chapter 7

LUV YA BLUE (AND WE LOVE *YOU*, TOO!)

From the time Oail Andrew Phillips Jr. first sauntered in with those cowboys boots and that cowboy hat, I knew this was a different type of head coach than any I ever saw before. That's the name his parents gave him, but thanks to his sister not being able to pronounce the word *brother,* we all know him as "Bum." Bum was my favorite head coach during my entire 16 years in the NFL. Most of the coaches I've admired in my life (Pat Clemens in high school, Hornsby Howell in college, and Wally Lemm and Sid Gillman in the NFL) had several things in common. Particularly they were all tough disciplinarians who worked their players hard and made it very clear who was the boss. When those guys yelled, "Jump!", we were expected to say, "How high?" Bum was a departure from that pattern for me in a lot of ways, but that's not to imply that he was weak. Easy-going, yes, but *never* weak.

Bum was elevated to the dual positions of head coach and general manager after the departure of Sid Gillman in 1975. He had been serving as our defensive coordinator, and he was really Coach Gillman's handpicked successor, but from the first day of training camp he immediately lightened the load. In fact, there was a fair amount of rejoicing from my teammates when Bum took over the Oilers.

When we arrived in Kerrville before the 1975 season, Bum made a big change that got the team's attention.

"We are not going to scrimmage during training camp," he announced. "Houston's not on our schedule so why should we play against ourselves in camp? We're preparing to play against the *rest* of the league, not the Oilers."

Who could argue with that logic?

I was an admirer of Coach Gillman, even though I agreed with the players who thought he practiced us too hard, but Bum's style made me see that respect and motivation could be instilled in a pro player without intimidation or fear.

We certainly got worked hard enough during Bum's practices, but he didn't let practices go too long. He also used some intriguing psychological techniques to get the best out of us. I remember a practice on one of the hottest dog days of the year where we were not concentrating well. After about 15 minutes, Bum ordered us back into the locker room.

"You're not doing anything out here!" he shouted. "You're just killing my grass."

He gave us a minute to get off the field, and we almost knocked each other down trying to get to that locker room. Even the injured guys were sprinting back inside. The psychology of Bum's order to end practice was very clever because we had a scrimmage the next day. Every guy on the team knew that we had better be great at that scrimmage because we were getting out early today. Bum could have worked us longer and harder in the heat, but he knew he'd get more out of us at the more important practice the following day.

Although Bum's coaching style was laid back, he knew each player's button and just how to push it for maximum results. It was the most amazing thing I ever saw. His people skills and his understanding of individual motivation techniques were second to none. We had some doozies on those Oiler teams, too. We had drunks, drug addicts, devil worshippers, egomaniacs, rednecks, and just about any type of varmint you wanted. We had saints and sinners, greats and near-greats, ingrates, and inmates. Bum handled them all perfectly. One time, two of our players were boarding a plane to come home after a game and they were obviously feeling no pain. Bum saw them and simply said, "Those guys are so high, they could catch ducks with a rake."

As a coach, he was willing to put up with a lot of crap from players. He had a very long fuse, and before he reached his breaking point with any player, he'd come to one of his favorite veterans—Dan Pastorini, Kenny Burrough, Carl Mauck, or me—and ask us to work the problem out on a peer-to-peer basis. He always told us we were the committee for taking care of these issues. If there was ever a situation that we couldn't take care of among ourselves, Bum would come in and do it, but we rarely ever let it get to that point.

He was enormously popular with the players because he knew how to reach them. Whenever our team was in a tight spot during a game, Bum looked at us and said simply, "Hold on to the rope, no matter how short it is." We must have heard that phrase a hundred times, but it got us through some tough situations, and it became such a trademark line for the players that we had "Hold on to the rope" T-shirts made. It inspired us, and we tried to stay in every game and fight to the last second, no matter how bleak it looked. We did our damnedest to hold on to that rope in every single game.

We were in New England for a game once and down by about 20 points at the half. In situations like that, I've witnessed head coaches throw raging tantrums, punching blackboards, kicking holes in the wall, and even worse. Bum treated us like professionals and adults. His remarks at halftime were simple but effective.

"Well, hell. This is not embarrassing me. You're the ones on the field. You're the ones that have to face the fans back in Houston. You're only embarrassing yourselves."

He didn't holler at us or berate us to get us back in that game, he just appealed to our egos and sense of professional pride. We eventually came back and won the game and avoided the humiliation.

He also didn't just inspire us with catchy phrases and his laid-back ways; he brought some real innovation. His decision to bring in Curley Culp at nose tackle was pure genius. Even though they never really hit it off, Bum got the absolute best out of Culp at a very difficult position. Culp made the difference in a lot of games, especially under Bum's 3-4 defensive front.

Bum even had a play named after him—"The Bummerooskie." It was a trick play that won at least one game for us (against the Chicago Bears in 1980) and involved setting up for a fake field goal, followed by an intentional fumble from the center, then a fullback sneak off tackle. It was a thing of beauty when it worked.

Bum Phillips was everything a professional player could ask for in a head coach, and I can't imagine having a better one. Man to man, our Oilers couldn't really match up with 75 percent of the teams in the league. Thanks to Bum's positive personality, he got the very best out of us, despite some shortcomings in actual talent. He didn't need to yell, scream, threaten, or conduct tortuous practices to get maximum performance and respect from his team. I was, and always will be, proud and honored to have played in the NFL for Bum Phillips.

The Luv Ya Blue era is easy to date on the timeline of Houston Oiler franchise history, because it coincides perfectly with the years that Bum was our head coach: 1975 to 1980. When Bum took over the reins in Houston, the love for the local football team was at an all-time low. Someone could have taken a box full of tickets for an Oiler home game and left them in the middle of the road, and not a single person would have picked them up. Hell, even the players had trouble getting people to take the extra tickets we had for games. But Bum's Texas-sized personality, coupled with an exciting inaugural season, changed everything and set off a phenomenon that completely overshadowed the labor of my first seven seasons with the Oilers. And to think it all started in 1975 with a handmade sign and an anonymous fan.

The 1975 season started quietly with the Oilers raking in wins against New England and San Diego. But a close 21-19 loss to the Bengals at home snapped the momentum we had built up. One Monday morning early in the 1975 season, we came to practice after a game and found ourselves celebrated in a unique way. Next to our practice facility was a medical building, and a nurse's aide, who worked there, had hung a hand-painted homemade banner in full view for the players to see. Emblazoned on the banner were the words "Luv Ya Blue," and every Monday morning after that (win, lose, or draw) her banner hung there to welcome us home and inspire us for the next round of battle on the gridiron. She gave us a boost every Monday morning and gave a little extra jolt to our practice motivation. She was a true fan, and I wish I knew her name.

Her motivation and Bum's personal touch led to a win on the road against Cleveland and a hard-hitting 13-10 win at home against quarterback Billy Kilmer and the Washington Redskins.

During the game rookie linebacker Robert Brazile, the epitome of smashmouth football and one of the best linebackers to ever play the game, made one of his most famous (or should that be infamous) plays. It was really a beauty to behold—well, unless you happened to be Billy Kilmer. For poor Kilmer, it was decidedly *not* beautiful. Brazile blitzed on a play, and all six feet, four inches and 240 pounds of him nailed Kilmer with an arm drag—more commonly known as a *clothesline*—just as he was throwing the ball. Kilmer's head went one way, and the helmet went the other. There was blood everywhere, flags flew, and a massive brawl broke out. Kilmer was knocked out of the game, but it was a quality clothesline. (If Brazile had done that today, he would have been fined $75,000 for the hit.)

Brazile's skill package was virtually unlimited. He could stuff the run, he could rush the passer, he could pursue from sideline to sideline, he could administer punishing tackles, and he could get just about anywhere he needed to be to make a play. For me, playing with Brazile was like being in a really tight jazz combo.

September 28, 1975. My 100th consecutive game in the NFL. The streak began with my first game as a rookie in 1968, and I played in 35 more consecutive games until I broke my arm in November 1977. I finished my career with 210 total games when I retired in 1983. My body hurts just thinking about it.
Lou Witt/Titans

We'd switch parts, we'd improvise, we'd instinctively get wherever we needed to be before the play even started, and we just made things happen together. Brazile played to my right, and we'd both race to see who could get to the other side of the field to catch the play before it got to the corner. This guy was just amazing to watch run.

Robert Brazile had it all—the height, the size, the agility, the speed, the athleticism, and perhaps most importantly, the killer instinct. They didn't call him "Dr. Doom" for nothing.

"Dr. Doom" and company continued to pound out the wins and as the wins racked up, we began to see Luv Ya Blue signs at games. Then there was a Luv Ya Blue song (sung to the tune of The Beatles' "Love Me Do") and before we knew what hit us, thousands of mass-produced pennants began to crop up around Houston after we capped a four-game win streak with wins against the Lions and the Chiefs. We went to Pittsburgh and lost 24-17, but there we saw Columbia Blue in the stands. We beat Miami and then lost to Pittsburgh again at home, but the signs stayed up. When we traveled to Cincinnati, there was another wave of blue even though we fell to the Bengals 23-19. In San Francisco and Oakland, the bright Columbia Blue cowboy hats were waving in the stands.

(One thing always stood out about playing in Oakland Coliseum. I called it "The Swamp," because the field was *always* wet. Our equipment manager would check the Oakland weather before we left for a road game there, and if the forecast was clear and dry, they'd pack our shoes with the short spikes. Then we'd land in Oakland, arrive at the Coliseum for the game, and the field was always soaking wet, but we didn't have our long spikes. I'm convinced they watered down that field before a game. Al Davis was always looking for an edge.)

Luv Ya Blue was infectious, and the team couldn't help getting caught up in it, too. I had never worn a cowboy hat in my life, but when the whole team got Columbia Blue cowboy hats, you better believe I wore one, too. Mike Barber, one of our tight ends, added the flourish of a pheasant feather to the back of his Luv Ya Blue cowboy hat, so the rest of us soon followed suit. Bum even had a pair of $900 ostrich cowboy boots in Columbia Blue, which he almost ruined by getting horse manure all over them at his ranch.

Luv Ya Blue fever swept through the country, and it was intoxicating to be the center of the attention. Steeler defensive lineman Joe Greene told me once that he thought the Oilers had the world by the ass during the Luv Ya Blue frenzy but that we didn't even know it. He was right. The poor lady who started the whole craze never imagined that it would be worth it to trademark her catchphrase. She threatened to sue but was placated by some season tickets. I don't think she ever got any money, but plenty of folks got rich selling Luv Ya Blue merchandise.

After closing our amazing season with a win over the Browns, we got to reflect on the incredible high of our 10-4 turnaround season. Bum deserved the credit for the turnaround because his coaching style and his relationships with players really made the difference. Our offense and defense seemed to be developing nicely. Players who had been brought in were maturing and becoming very influential in our game plan, as well as making names for themselves on the national scene.

One player was Billy "White Shoes" Johnson. When the Oilers drafted this little bespectacled halfback in 1974 from Widener College in the 15th round, we didn't expect too much from him at all. Sid Gillman, our head coach/general manager at the time, wasn't even too thrilled about the pick. He dismissed Johnson as a "midget."

"White Shoes" was just sensational. He brought so much electricity and excitement to the Houston Oilers and really the entire NFL. Johnson brought those trademark white shoes, which earned him his nickname, but he brought the kind of speed and aggressive moves that turned kick returning into an offensive weapon.

Before too long, there were guys on the Oilers who were begging to be on the kick return team after we saw what Johnson could do. Every time he touched the ball, there was a chance that he'd score a touchdown. He was going to make the opposing defenders look bad, and if they didn't stop him, he was going to get six points fast and perform one of his trademark end zone dances, a celebration he introduced to the NFL. He'd knock his knees together in a butterfly move, do a split, or even fake-toss the ball into the stands. We learned we should wait until his dance was over before running in the end zone to congratulate him. Unlike Randy Moss or Terrell Owens today, Johnson's dances were always just a celebration of the touchdown and not a means of embarrassing the opposing team or its fans. It was a natural extension of the euphoria he felt after a great kick return for a score. I can only imagine what "White Shoes" thinks of the spectacles that go on in end zones these days.

"White Shoes" Johnson was enormously popular with his teammates, and he was an incredibly humble guy who never turned down an autograph request from a fan.

The euphoria surrounding the Oilers in 1975 was hard to believe. Going into the next season our fans expected the same things: highlight plays and big wins. We opened the season with wins over the Buccaneers and the Bills before we fell to the Raiders in a game that went down to the wire. The Luv Ya Blue fever was still in tact when we headed to New Orleans to play the Saints.

Things got a little rowdy against the Saints that day, thanks to Zeke Moore, my co-conspirator on defense. Moore was a very dirty player whose forte was eye-poking. During the Saints game as he was wrestling with Saint wide receiver Tinker Owens, he stuck his big hand inside Owens's facemask to gouge him.

No sooner did Moore make contact, then the flags flew and the Saints' offense charged, starting a fight right around the scene of the crime. The wave of boos from the gold and black fans was deafening as the referee removed Moore from the game and placed him on the sideline.

At the time Owens was the hottest thing going in New Orleans, and even though the referee had ejected Moore from the game, the fans were very upset about his disregard for the eyesight of their favorite son. They decided to express their displeasure with more than boos. As Moore stood on the sidelines, the fans started to pelt him with pennies, oranges, and anything that wasn't nailed down. The ref noticed the hailstorm and instructed him to leave before someone got hurt.

As Moore made his way out of the stadium and down the ramp to the locker room, an apple—the chosen missile of an angered fan—hit him on the head and fell at his feet. Moore, in his typically defiant way, picked up the apple, took a bite out of it, and threw it back in the stands.

That was Zeke Moore. He was hardcore.

(As a side note, Zeke was my roommate for years, and it's a miracle I survived. One year he came to training camp right after there had been some race riots near his home in Alabama. For some reason, he had brought a sawed-off shotgun with him.

"Where did you get that, Zeke?" a teammate asked innocently.

"We took it from a cop car during the riots," Zeke replied nonchalantly.

Our jaws dropped.

"You did what?!?" the shocked teammate responded. "Well, what are you going to do it with it now?!?"

"We're going to shoot chi-chi birds," Moore answered casually.

There is practically no meat on a chi-chi bird, and it would take about 50 of them to make a meal, but that was Zeke Moore.)

After the fuss and a 31-26 win in New Orleans, we played Denver in the Astrodome and beat them 17-3. We were 4-1, and it looked like Luv Ya Blue would continue on forever when we went to face the Chargers in San Diego.

We lost a close one on that road trip to San Diego, and the loss seemed to pull our legs out from under us because our opponents edged us in eight out of the next nine games. Luv Ya Blue had lost some of its luster with a disappointing 5-9 performance. I thought the Oilers had changed. I loved playing for Bum, I especially loved the energy that the Luv Ya Blue concept brought to the Oilers, but it began to look like all of these things were just fleeting and that we might be going back down the same losing spiral all over again.

The 5-9 season slapped me in the face, and after playing out my option in 1976, the Oilers were holding out on offering me a deal. Now, I had a reputation for being disgruntled about contracts year after year, but I just wanted to earn a fair market price for my value to the team. I was looking to earn a salary that was comparable to the salaries of other players around the league who were playing at my level. Because I was making All-Pro and going to Pro Bowls regularly, I thought it was reasonable to expect compensation that reflected those honors. The Oilers weren't agreeing with that assessment apparently, so I began to consider other options. I talked with some friends, and Art Shell and Gene Upshaw, two of the Raiders' future Hall of Fame offensive linemen, began to grease the wheels for me with Al Davis, who was coming off his Super Bowl XI win, shortly before the 1977 season started.

As all of this was going on, I made the required 24-hour appearances every three days at Oiler training camp in Nacogdoches, so I could still get paid. I sat on the side of the hill wearing my big sombrero and watched my teammates practice. I ate dinner in the dining hall and then drove back to Houston for three days until I needed to appear again. It was my own personal strike. Every couple of days the management and I came to the bargaining table for negotiations, but nothing happened. It was at a standstill that was going to take some drastic movement on either side to get me back to the team.

Bum showed his creative side and came up with a plan to help bridge the gap between my proposals and the team's offers.

"Hey, Elvin, Bud and I have this cattle deal in Amarillo, and I think you should look into joining us," he suggested.

"What do I know about cattle? I'm from Trenton, New Jersey," I reminded him.

Bum smiled and said he would explain it to me, which he tried to do. He told me about hedging and cattle and how they can only stay in the feedlot for 90 days—but I didn't really understand what he was saying.

"You could probably make an additional $80,000 a year," he concluded.

I looked at him and thought, "If Bum is already in it, I guess that is good enough for me."

I ended the preliminary negotiations with the Raiders and signed a contract for the salary that the Oilers were offering with the idea that this cattle deal would put things over the top for me. Life was good and I was set. I was once again a Houston Oiler.

Well, a few months later the termination date of the feedlot contract came and went, but I never received a check. Eventually I got a call from Lad Herzeg, the Oilers' general manager at the time, who wanted me to come over and sign my check from the cattle deal. I had a smile on my face all of the way to his office as I pictured the number on that piece of paper.

I walked into Herzeg's office, and he showed me all of the facts and figures relating to the cattle scheme. He explained how much we got for selling the cattle, and then Herzeg handed me the check for $80,000.

"Just sign it and give it back to me," he explained.

"Well, why?" I asked puzzled.

He explained that the price of beef had gone down so much that it had become more expensive to keep 200 to 300 heads of cattle than to just sell them and take the loss. It had eaten up all of my profits. I got nothing. I signed the check, tore it up, and then threw the pieces at him. We had a saying on the team back then, which I shouldn't have ignored: "How can you tell when Lad Herzeg is lying? His lips are moving."

I was really mad at myself though, because I should have never gone into the deal without a lawyer, and I really should have properly educated myself before signing anything I didn't understand.

(In the end there's something poetic about the fact that it was a cattle deal with Bud Adams that seems to be my most famous NFL contract negotiation. Before free agency, NFL players were, in effect, just branded cattle themselves. My brand was the Houston Oilers. If one of us was traded or released or retired, then another one was brought in with a different name and number on the same jersey. That's just the way it was on every team.)

Do I regret not becoming a Raider? It might have meant winning a Super Bowl or two, and maybe even getting into the Hall of Fame sooner. Well, the Man Upstairs had a better idea for me than becoming an Oakland Raider, but that doesn't mean it hasn't crossed my mind from time to time.

One of the first people I met in 1977 after I ended my hold-out was our new placekicker, Toni Fritsch. Fritsch never looked much like a football player—he was only five feet, seven inches tall and 180 pounds. He also never quite got the hang of genuine NFL trash talk, either. When Fritsch wanted to insult someone, he'd say, "Bethea, you are a Communist!" He was a cool guy to be around, though, and everyone on the team just loved him.

Bum used to say, "Every time I look at [Fritsch], I thank God for our immigration laws." If the ball was anywhere near the end zone on fourth down and you asked Fritsch if he thought he could kick the field goal from there, his answer was always the same—"No problem." Just imagine that line being uttered in a thick Austrian accent and you've got an idea what he was like.

The 1977 season was a roller-coaster ride of wins and losses. We won two against the Jets and the Packers, and then lost to the Dolphins in Miami. We picked ourselves back up with a 27-10 win over the Steelers, only to lose the next three games before pounding the Bears 47-0.

We journeyed to Oakland with a 4-4 record, and my preseason contract flirtation with the Raiders took an interesting twist. I went into that game having played in 135 consecutive games. The streak was in tact until I met Raider running back Mark Van Eeghen—or rather I met his helmet. During one play, he came around my end on a run, and I tried to bring him down with a well-placed forearm clothesline. Van Eeghen ducked his head at just the wrong time—or the right time for him—and my arm went crashing into silver and black. I crumpled over in pain. I had a compound fracture, which took me out of the next couple of games. I ended the season fully equipped with a cast that seems to appear in every photo of me from that year.

The 1977 season was an improvement on the backward slide we had experienced in 1976. The Oilers finished with a respectable 8-6 record, which was good enough for second place in the AFC Central Division. We were second, of course, right behind the Pittsburgh Steelers.

The Luv Ya Blue years were such a laugh after all of the years of losing. We were able to balance having fun and kicking back with playing hard-hitting competitive football. Before we were the nobodies of the NFL in a town that the press cared very little about; during Luv Ya Blue we became Houston's darlings, and the press coverage that followed was more friendly and amicable than it had been in the downtimes of the late 1960s and early 1970s. For example, we always had a charter plane for road games, and initially the first-team starters sat in first class, and the rest of the team, along with corporate sponsors, front-office employees, and the press corps all sat in coach. Before too long, the first team decided it was a lot more fun to be in the back of the plane with the reporters. We announced to Adams that we thought it was best if everyone just sat wherever they wanted, and so we did. Someone was always on the microphone fooling around back then, so one day, while we were waiting for a reporter to board before we took off, I got on the mike and asked, "Is all the riff-raff on board yet so we can leave?" The nickname "riff-raff" stuck and, to this day, all of my friends in the press proudly wear their titles of riff-raff.

My best buddies in the media were Bob Allen, Dave Ward, John McClain, Ron Stone, Harold Lundgren, and Ron Franklin. I liked them all, but Ward was my drinking partner, so he was my main riff-raff. The per diem for our meals back then was always two five dollar bills and two one dollar bills, plus we got two ice-cold cans of Coors beer when we walked on the plane to head home. The players who didn't drink would give their beer away, so the drinkers got very good at boarding the plane right next to the non-drinkers. (In the latter years of my playing career, I started bringing along a bottle of scotch to make the flight home go a bit smoother. That bottle of scotch made me even more popular than the guys who gave away their two cans of Coors.

Unfortunately, a $12 per diem didn't even pay for my fifth of scotch, much less a decent meal.)

Most of the time the team got along well with the media from the Luv Ya Blue era, But there were some reporters who still harped on the negatives even after we had won, and that was soul-crushing for us as a team. Barry Warner of KIKK Radio was a prime example of a consistently negative media type who never seemed to find anything good about our efforts on the field. According to Warner's on-air columns, Bud Adams could do nothing right, Bum Phillips could do nothing right, and nothing the team did was ever right. Well, one time, I got pissed off about something he had said on the air, and I happened to run into him in our locker room, nipping around my teammates' ankles like a little chihuahua. Like a sheriff from the old West, I sauntered over to Warner, who was standing near Bum, and looked him up and down.

"I should throw you into our whirlpool for being so negative," I growled at him.

"Elvin, don't do it!" Bum warned. "You could get sued!"

As I stood there and looked at him, it was just too irresistible. Despite my coach's pleas, I scooped up Warner like a baby and lowered him gently into the water with a plop. There he was up to his chest in water soaking wet. He should probably consider himself lucky. I was proud of myself for exercising so much restraint—I really wanted to hold him by his ankles and let him soak underwater for an hour or so.

The 1978 season brought us Earl Campbell. Such a simple sentence, but it meant the world to us. Campbell was the determining factor in our success in 1978 and 1979. We had all of the other pieces of the puzzle in place, but he just put us over the top. The story goes that Bum decided we needed a back like Earl Campbell after Franco Harris had a great game against the Oilers midway through the 1975 season. Apparently, Bum figured a back like Harris was just what the Oilers needed to put us in the playoff hunt.

"I wanted other coaches to have to face that kind of punishing back every week," he told us.

As usual, Bum was right about the prescription for the Oilers' success.

When Campbell showed up, the offense was built around the speed and strength of his running game. Tight end Mike Barber became an effective blocker for Campbell but at the same time was able to use his quickness to develop his receiving skills to where he became one of Dante's favorite targets—when he wasn't taking the quarterback's girls. Both men were popular with the ladies, so we'd see them fighting over the same women from time to time. In fact, there was a story around the locker room that Dan didn't throw to Barber for two games after Barber stole away one of Pastorini's girlfriends. I'm not sure I believe that story, though, because how could anyone steal a woman away from Dan Pastorini?!?

At the time, Barber also was a stone cold redneck. He wouldn't even shower in front of the "brothers." After practice, he ran as fast as he could into the locker room and got his shower done by the time we got in there. As the rest of us got to the showers, Barber was already dressed and halfway out the front door. Of course, when we were playing on the road, he was stuck with us. (Barber now runs a prison ministry and brings the gospel to jailhouses all across the country. Whatever his views on the world may have been back in our Oiler years, it takes a special person to do that kind of difficult work, and Barber has every reason to be proud of it.)

Thanks to the blocking of Barber and the offensive line, Campbell gained more than 5,000 yards on the ground, and scored 45 touchdowns, over the course of his first three seasons with the Oilers (1978-1980). Campbell had thighs like tree trunks, and considering the punishment he took on the field, it's amazing that he only missed six games during his entire career. Watching him and marveling at the things he could do on the field was an exhilarating part of the fabric of late 1970s NFL football. He deserved all of the press and awards that he got, but I'll admit to being a bit envious of the attention that he received. It's embarrassing to admit that, but, after all, I had been busting my ass in the trenches of some pretty horrible Oiler teams for almost 10 years, and at times, I felt like I deserved a medal for still being there. As teammates, Campbell and I weren't especially close, but Campbell was the one who turned the key that got us in the door to the playoffs. I was delighted that there was a light in the wilderness when Campbell came to town.

It did take a little bit of time for Campbell to make an impact. The 1978 season kicked off with a loss to the Falcons and tight wins over the Chiefs and the 49ers. The next game was the one where Campbell proved he was going to be hard to take down.

We were playing the Los Angeles Rams in the fourth game of the 1978 season. Campbell had the ball, and he smashed the Rams' All-Pro linebacker, Isiah Robertson, flat on his back. He just lowered his shoulder and drove Robertson back like a grown man playing against little boys. In the same game, he dragged a safety for about eight yards and put a serious hurt on Jack Youngblood, a future Hall of Fame defensive end. We lost that game to the Rams 10-6, but it sent a message to the rest of the league.

The Oilers were riding a two-game winning streak later in the season when we played the Dolphins on *Monday Night Football*. It was a phenomenal game, one of the best I have ever experienced. We were tied at 14-14 at the half, and then we were at 21-21 after the third quarter. It was anybody's game late in the fourth quarter until Campbell took a pitchout from Pastorini and sprinted down the sidelines for an 80-yard touchdown run. We won 35-30, and Campbell ended the night with 199 yards rushing and four touchdowns. It was that game, in my opinion, that put the Houston Oilers on the map as a force to be reckoned with in the NFL. The league was now on notice that we meant business and we had a star running back who could be a game breaker.

Although we made the playoffs in 1978, we were the wild-card team, which meant we couldn't make any mistakes. Our regular-season record of 10-6 may have been a little deceptive, because every one of those 10 wins was a close game. In fact our opponents outscored us that season to the tune of about 300-285. It's fair to say that we were not perceived as a powerhouse team in the AFC, nor were we expected to get very far in the playoffs. But none of those realities seemed to matter to us when we arrived in Miami to play on Christmas Eve. This was the Oilers' first playoff game in about 10 years, so the team was hyped up, our fans were hyped up, and the national media was making it very clear that we had no chance to beat the Dolphins, especially in Miami. There was our key to victory—just telling us we *couldn't* do it was the extra motivation we needed.

We were so relaxed that even Bum was dancing in the locker room before the game. There was music playing from every corner of that locker room—R&B, reggae, country and western, rock 'n' roll—and Bum just made the rounds, saying something encouraging to every single guy on the team. The anxiety of being in a playoff game for the first time had us so psyched up that we actually began to embrace this seemingly impossible challenge. We were eager to be tested at this higher level because everyone had already written us off. No one expected the Oilers, a wildcard team, to go any further, and we were faced with having to win three consecutive games against the conference's best teams on their home turf just to get the chance to play in the

Super Bowl against the NFC's best team, which was shaping up to be the Cowboys.

Dan was pretty banged up for the Miami game. He had been in the hospital all week with a strain in his hamstring, a banged-up knee, a bruised elbow, and a few broken ribs. It was foolish to even consider that he could play that week, but some guy had invented a special flak jacket that Dante could wear to protect his injured body for the big game. I watched him put on each of these special pads that covered his entire torso. He stood tall, bound completely around his middle. Then I watched as the inventor took an aluminum baseball bat and pounded on my friend to test the jacket. Dan didn't feel anything. Now that he was suited up, he was ready to play.

Armed with some protection for his three broken ribs but still dealing with a bad knee and a sore elbow, Pastorini threw for more than 300 yards in that game. (*That's* a smashmouth warrior, if there ever was one.) Burrough and Barber each had more than 100 yards receiving, and our defense forced five turnovers. Miami was tough, though, and they were playoff veterans, so we were in a 7-7 tie going into the fourth quarter. Then Fritsch kicked a field goal, and Campbell punched one in from the one-yard line. The final score was 17-9, and we finally felt like we were *somebody*. We may have been mutts, but we played like purebreds that night. It felt like we had just won the Super Bowl, and needless to say, our flight home was a wild party.

The following week on New Year's Eve, we were at Foxboro Stadium taking on the New England Patriots. My personal challenge was getting past an awesome offensive line tandem of Leon Gray and John Hannah—two of the best I've ever faced. Then I had to handle Steve Grogan, one of the league's most reliable quarterbacks that season. If you looked at these two teams, the Oilers and the Patriots, and analyzed them man to man, it was another game we shouldn't have won. Pastorini, Burrough, and

Barber just shredded the Pats' defense to the extent that we entered the half with a 21-0 lead. The second half was just Campbell running at them almost nonstop. It hardly seems possible, but we had an easy win and polished off New England by a score of 31-14. We felt hotter than hot. How could we lose? The game at Foxboro convinced us that we now could win it all.

We were one win away from the Super Bowl, but we had to get past the Pittsburgh Steelers in the AFC championship game. We had played the Steelers twice during the regular season and beat them once in Pittsburgh, so we knew it could be done. There were nine future Hall of Famers on that Steeler team (Terry Bradshaw, Lynn Swann, John Stallworth, Franco Harris, Mike Webster, Mel Blount, Jack Ham, Jack Lambert, and Joe Greene), a future Hall of Fame head coach (Chuck Noll), and a slew of other players who were All-Pros or Pro Bowl regulars (Rocky Bleier, Roy Gerela, L.C. Greenwood, Donnie Shell, and Dwight White). Still, in spite of all evidence to the contrary, we were confident that we matched up well against them, and we all believed in the probability of an Oiler upset on January 7 in Pittsburgh.

The weather in Pittsburgh was wet, sloppy, and freezing cold. Their offensive line, led by their dominant center Mike Webster, was trying to psyche us out by playing with bare arms in that bitter winter weather. Whether it was the climate, the Steelers' containment of Campbell, the Oilers' porous defense, or the Oilers' nine turnovers, we were losing 31-3 at the half. As Bum said, "The behinder we got, the worse it got." At halftime the coaches all gave lip service to the things we should do in the second half to turn the game around, but we had never come back from a deficit that large before.

The guys on my side of the ball were convinced that the offense couldn't win this game for us, so the defense had to do it by getting turnovers. We were trying so hard to make something

Terry Bradshaw completed more than 2,000 passes in the NFL. I am happy to report that this was not one of them because I am about to swat it down.
Lou Witt/Titans

dramatic happen that we took a lot of gambles and made some mistakes. I'm still proud of the fact that our defense kept the Steelers to a field goal in the second half, and we even scored a safety.

Toward the end of the game, Bum told the first team to stay on the sidelines when it was time for the defense to be on the field. Curley Culp and I looked at each other, grabbed our helmets, and told the younger guys in our position to go back to the sideline. We didn't want to miss a second of that game, especially if there was the tiniest hope that we could make a difference.

It was too little, too late. The damage had been done, and we slinked away from Pittsburgh with a 34-5 loss.

That horrible Pittsburgh weather caused a three-hour delay at the airport for our return flight. As I sat on the plane waiting for it to take off, I thought about the Steelers. I always looked forward to playing against Pittsburgh because of all of the big names on their team. They were our biggest division rivals, but they were also the ultimate test due to the world-class talent on the field. The Steelers seemed to have switches on their backs that they could flip to *on*. The playoffs would come along, and they'd just barrel down everything in their path.

I also thought about the pep rally that was waiting for us in Houston. It had been organized to be held, win or lose, at the Astrodome when we got back to Houston. "There won't be many fans there now," I thought. "Who was going to be showing up at the Dome after midnight to rally any pep on behalf of a losing team?"

I underestimated our Houston fans.

There were mobs of people waiting for the team at Houston Intercontinental Airport when we arrived. You'd have thought that some Hollywood stars were landing. We loaded onto two buses and headed to the Astrodome, but the traffic was so jammed around the stadium that we had to get out and walk the last several hundred yards. We entered the field of the Astrodome to find 60,000 screaming Oiler fans waiting to honor their losing team. There was a stage assembled, and speeches were made, but I couldn't tell you what was said. I remember the huge cloud of gray cigarette smoke that hovered at the top of the Dome. I remember one of the mounted police officers pulling Robert Brazile onto his horse and riding with him around the Dome to the delight of the fans. I remember thinking it was the highlight of my life.

I couldn't wait for the 1979 season so that we could give Houston something to *really* cheer about. Back then, we didn't get paid for offseason workouts, as they do now, but we knew we had something very exciting to build upon for 1979 so we all got working early. I followed my usual regimen of total rest during January and then got back to weight training in February. Most of my teammates, even those who normally didn't work out in the offseason, did the same. We wanted to be ready to take the Houston Oilers all the way in 1979.

The offseason also brought some exciting new blood to our team. One of the happiest days of my life was when the New England Patriots traded Leon Gray to the Houston Oilers. Prior to that trade I had to face Gray—who is at least in the top three offensive linemen I have ever faced—in tandem with John Hannah, for five years of sheer hell. Gray had everything—the best footwork, the best balance, the greatest strength. I can't describe him better than that. Very few people seem to remember him these days, but if you played against him on the line, you'd never forget him. If I had been forced to face Gray as an opponent every week, you would not be reading this book. I would have become a physical therapist and moved back to North Carolina.

We also got defensive back Vernon Perry from the Canadian Football League in 1979. For some reason, he couldn't (or

If I were to hazard a guess as to what's going through the mind of Jet quarterback Richard Todd, it would probably be—"Why did Joe Namath have to retire?" **Lou Witt/Titans**

wouldn't) say "Elvin" and always called me "Albin." Perry was a practical joker who was always putting something in someone's shoe. He'd come into a game walking like Fred Sanford and crack everybody up. He was just always doing something stupid. And even though he kept things just as loose on the field as he did in the locker room, Perry was always right there to make a play. That gave us one more reason to like him.

We chugged right along at a pretty impressive winning pace throughout the regular season. We looked great in some high-profile games, too. We beat the Dolphins in Miami in a 9-6 squeaker on *Monday Night Football*. We demolished the Bengals in Houston 42-21 and beat a very tough Oakland team 31-17.

Then came Thanksgiving Day in Dallas. The Oilers had never beaten the Cowboys in a regular-season game. This was the third meeting of the two Texas teams for a game when it really counted in the standings. Adding to the pressure was the fact that it was a nationally televised holiday game. We were down 21-10 when Gray made two plays that turned the game around for us. The first one came when we had a second-and-10 from deep in our territory. Gray's blocking assignment was Harvey Martin, the Cowboys' All-Pro defensive end. Martin made a dash for Pastorini on a pass play, but Gray reacted with a brilliant move to shove him aside at the very last second. Pastorini then completed a 30-yard pass to Rich Caster at midfield. Later in the drive, Gray knocked Martin out of the way a second time and held off the Dallas linebackers so Campbell could dash past them all for a 25-yard touchdown run, which pulled us even closer. After we scored again, Dallas was beating us 24-23 in the fourth quarter when Pastorini connected with Burrough for a 30-yard touchdown pass. We won 30-24.

The final big test of the regular season was our second *Monday Night Football* game of the year—this time at the Astrodome against the Pittsburgh Steelers. We took on the

Steelers before a sold-out crowd of screaming Houston fans. Campbell ran for 109 yards against the Steel Curtain, and we beat them 20-17. We ended the 1979 season with a record of 11-5, just enough for another wildcard berth, but not enough to win the AFC Central Division. The Steelers finished 12-4 and were in the driver's seat again.

Finishing second in the AFC Central meant we were going to need to win four playoff games, including the Super Bowl, to finish the season as champions. We knew we could do it. Our first task was to take on the Broncos at Mile High Stadium. We lost Campbell with a pulled groin after taking a 10-7 lead against Denver. Then Pastorini and Burrough were knocked out of the game with injuries. It was up to the defense to hold the Broncos to those seven little points. We had to hold them, because we weren't convinced we had enough offensive firepower left to score again.

The Oilers' defense answered the call. We sacked Broncos quarterback Craig Morton six times and forced two interceptions to stay alive with a 13-7 victory.

We turned to face the Chargers in San Diego the next Sunday. The main question was, "Could we get our three best offensive weapons healthy enough to suit up for the game?" The answer came back as a resounding "No." Based on the severity of their injuries, we couldn't get them healthy enough for the game. So, without Pastorini, Burrough, and Campbell, would we have any chance of winning against one of the most dangerous and potent offenses in the NFL? Yes! Even though our offense was anemic behind Giff Nielsen at quarterback and Rob Carpenter at running back, we thought we still could win as we prepared to face the Chargers the next week. The media didn't give us much hope of survival against Dan Fouts's Chargers, and when Fouts sliced through our secondary with a touchdown on their opening drive, it looked even bleaker for the Boys in Blue.

Then the Oiler defense decided to hold a clinic.

Perry blocked a Charger field-goal attempt, and thanks to a field goal of our own from Toni Fritsch and a touchdown from fullback Bobbie Clark, we were leading 10-7 at the half. In the second half, Lydell Mitchell ran for another touchdown for San Diego, but Mike Renfro caught one for us.

That was it as far as scoring went. Perry intercepted Fouts four times, and I sacked Fouts another four times. We did the impossible on two fronts—we held the explosive Chargers' offense to only 14 points and managed to get 17 points of our own without our three offensive superstars in the game.

We were riding a wave of momentum that seemed unbeatable when we found ourselves in Pittsburgh for our second consecutive AFC championship game against the Steelers.

Our defense got things off to a roaring start in that historic game. Perry intercepted Bradshaw very early and ran it back for a 75-yard touchdown. Fritsch got a field goal a bit later, and we were up 10-7 in the second quarter. It was foolish to believe that you could keep the Steelers' offense quiet forever, and Bradshaw would not be denied in a big game. Bradshaw threw for two touchdowns, and at halftime, we went into the locker room down 17-10.

No one in our locker room was worried, though. We were clearly still in it, I reminded myself at halftime, and our defense had proved in San Diego and elsewhere that we could be game breakers. Plus, we had Pastorini, Campbell, and Burrough at full strength. True, Pittsburgh was stacking the line against Campbell so he was not making a big difference in this game thus far, but Pastorini had Renfro, Burrough, and Barber available to do some damage in the air. When the gun sounded for the start of the third quarter, we were ready to show the country we had in it us to beat the Steelers.

It was shortly into the third when the hinges fell off for us. Actually, it wasn't just the hinges; the doorknob came flying off, too. We thought we had it tied in the third when Pastorini connected with Renfro for a touchdown in the back of the end zone. Pastorini lobbed it in perfectly, Renfro pulled it down by his fingertips, and then Ron Johnson, the Steelers' defensive back, pushed Renfro out of bounds. The officials all got together after the play and discussed whether Renfro had possession when he crossed the end line. Finally, after an interminable delay, the refs couldn't be sure if Renfro's feet were out of bounds or that he had sufficient possession of the ball, so they ruled it an incomplete pass. Bum was understandably furious, and he protested, for all the good it did.

NBC ran endless replays, but they weren't conclusive. Football fans all across the country seemed to believe they saw a touchdown catch, and that the Oilers were robbed. Later I spoke with Jim Tunney, the dean of NFL referees who was officiating that game, and he confided in me that he was sure Renfro made the catch but had been overruled by the ref who was in position for the play. I have since seen the play from another angle on the NFL Network, and it shows Renfro catching the ball with both of his feet in the end zone and then dragging them out. It remains one of the most debated plays in NFL history, and it's largely responsible for the institution of the instant replay in NFL games in 1986.

The Renfro touchdown catch would have taken us into the fourth quarter with a 17-17 tie and would have been just the shot in the arm we needed. Instead, we had to settle for a field goal. We lost our momentum. We lost it to the Steelers that day 27-13.

After the game I had tears in my eyes in the locker room. I was convinced that it was over for us in the postseason.

"That's it," I thought, "We'll never get back again."

The Steelers always seemed to be one step ahead of us in our division.
George Gojkovich/Getty Images

I hated being pessimistic, but I just thought that our time in the sun had come and gone.

I've been asked over the years what it felt like to be a perennial bridesmaid to the Steelers when it came to every postseason of the 1970s. No one expressed that feeling better for me than the Texas sports journalist Bob Hulsey, who wrote, "If you ever had a next-door neighbor that won the lottery, married the prettiest girl in town, and drove a Ferrari, you'd know how the Oilers felt being in the same division with the Pittsburgh Steelers." You said it, Bob. We might have been the second-best team in the whole league, after the Steelers, but because we shared the same division, we never seemed to get anything but local coverage.

After we got home to Houston, there was another celebration at the Astrodome. It was even bigger than the previous year's, if that was possible. The Dome was filled to overflowing, and thousands of Oiler fan were turned away. But for me it was bittersweet because I felt we'd never get this close again. I didn't want to be right, but unfortunately, I was. Those two playoffs were the greatest ride I ever had in the pros. Those 1978 and 1979 seasons were the pinnacle of my entire NFL life. Those Oiler teams of mine were a bunch of characters, but we had *character,* too. We won more games and went farther in the postseason than anyone thought we would. I was proud of my teammates, my coaches, and even myself. On those two nights of incredible celebration in the Dome after our playoff losses, I was proud of the Houston fans, too.

I don't remember any of the speeches made that night, except for one. Bum came up with one of the most memorable quotes in Houston sports history when he summed it all up for 60,000 screaming, yelling, and cheering delirious Houston Oiler fans.

"One year ago, we knocked on the door. This year, we beat on the door. Next year, we're gonna kick the son of a bitch in!"

I watched him finish his speech and thought about those words.

"I hope Bum knows something I don't."

The following season turned out to be a pretty good one. We added some new faces to our unit who continued the Oiler tradition of being solid characters. One of the new additions was defensive back Jack Tatum, a quiet guy. Tatum was a former Raider who seemed to scare the entire team. You just never knew if something was going to click in Tatum's head during a practice. The guys were terrified because if something *did* click, he just might take somebody out. I liked that. I also liked Tatum's afro. He combed his hair straight back so it made him look like a cross between Dracula and the Wolfman. That's what we would call stylin'.

On one of our plane trips back to Houston after a road game, Tatum, who never socialized on the plane, pulled a blanket over his head so he could sleep in his seat. Some of the guys were drinking too much and were going from person to person on the plane yelling, "Wake up! Wake up!" Naturally, it was designed to be annoying, and it worked. Well, when they got to Tatum, who was hidden underneath the blanket, and woke him up, they suddenly got real apologetic and fearful when he peeked out.

"It's okay, Jack," one mumbled humbly.

"You go back to sleep," another said soothingly. "We're sorry, Jack."

That's how terrified Jack Tatum could make everyone.

Another new Oiler was Ken "The Snake" Stabler, who came to the Oilers in 1980 as part of a trade that sent my buddy Dan Pastorini to the Raiders. Dante was much younger than Stabler and had a cannon for an arm, but Stabler was probably more accurate than Dan, and "The Snake" had a Super Bowl ring to his credit. When everything was tallied on each side, it seemed like a wash, at least professionally. On the personal side, it was tough to lose a great friend like Dante Pastorini.

"The Snake" was a swashbuckling wild man. He was only 35 years old when the Oilers got him, but his gray hair made him look 10 years older. Stabler lived life to the fullest (and beyond), and he was a real piece of work, in the best sense of that phrase. It's no secret that Stabler loved the liquid and the ladies. He had been a big winner in Oakland and distinguished himself as one of the better quarterbacks in the league, but by the time he got to Houston, he was on his last legs. "The Snake" was a real crowd-pleaser in Houston, and it made all of our lives more interesting to have him on the team.

In 1980, we finished 11-5 (again), but the Steelers finished 12-4 (again). We were the wildcard team (again), but there was no fairytale ride to the AFC championship game in Pittsburgh this time. We lost 27-7 at Oakland in the wildcard game, and our season was over just like that. The Raiders went on to win Super Bowl XV that year and became the first wildcard team to go all the way. (If you think that I didn't wonder again how my professional life might have been different if I went to the Raiders in 1977, then you're wrong. Better yet, I really just wished that my Oilers had been the first wildcard team to go all the way in either 1978 or 1979.)

After the 1980 season, things came to a grinding halt. I played in my last of eight Pro Bowls, and Bum left the Oilers to become head coach of the New Orleans Saints, taking half of the coaching staff with him. My friend Eddie Biles, the Oilers' defensive coordinator, became the new head coach, and because Adams had announced to the press that his primary reason for firing our trusted coach was that Bum had refused to hire an offensive coordinator, Coach Biles wasted no time hiring himself an offensive coordinator.

Ed Biles was a great defensive coordinator and is still a good friend of mine to this day. I think he would agree that he probably should have never tried to be a head coach. Although he certainly knew the game and everyone respected his abilities as a defensive strategist, I saw that a lot of my teammates lost respect for Coach Biles when he got the promotion. Some of the Oiler veterans resented being given curfews and having fines levied by Biles, but I was not one of them. I've always been a big fan of discipline on a football team, and I never lost respect for him when he became our head coach.

The result of this lack of respect was a 7-9 season, and that was the high point in Eddie Biles's head coaching tenure. The Luv Ya Blue era was essentially over. I was never to play in another winning NFL season and never to play in another postseason game again.

Chapter 8

THE HILLS ARE ALIVE (WITH THE SOUND OF GUINEA PIGS)

n April 1982, I received an offer that I couldn't resist. The NFL Players Association was tying in with great organizations such as CARE, a nonprofit humanitarian organization, so that we could give back to the world community in a positive visible way. There was a false impression then, as there also is now, that all NFL players were selfish, greedy goons. Uniting our players' association with CARE served a dual purpose. Most importantly, we got the unbelievable opportunity to make a huge difference in the Third World by helping to fight global poverty with one of the planet's foremost humanitarian groups. But we also got the chance to help rehabilitate our league's public image with good works. To me, the decision to participate with CARE was a no-brainer. For one thing, I always wanted to see the world, especially places where the cultures and language were vastly different from the United States.

Plus, anytime I'm offered the chance to help children, I'm there.

We got our assignment from CARE. There were seven of us from the NFL who were being sent to Peru. I would be joined by Guy Benjamin (a quarterback with the 49ers), Ray Ellis (a defensive back with the Eagles), Christopher Godfrey (an offensive lineman with the Jets), Sam McCullum (a wide receiver with the Vikings), Beasley Reece (a defensive back with the Giants), and Benny Ricardo (a placekicker with the Saints). It was an interesting mix of personalities, and everyone's heart seemed to be in the right place for this adventure. None of us was a superstar; we were just hard-working NFL guys. A project manager from CARE met with us to map out the practical purpose of our Peruvian visit. The manager explained that the women in these villages were forced to walk miles to bring water back to their families. The villages toward the top of the Andes naturally got the freshest water. As the water made its way downhill, it got nastier and nastier. People urinated in it, animals defecated in it, and because it was just an open stream, there was no way of knowing all of the sickening things that were dumped in it. Aside from serving as ambassadors for the NFL, we were going to be demonstrating modern methods for getting and holding fresh water in the villages of the Andes Mountains. By introducing the notion of holding tanks and water purification, we were hoping to make life healthier and happier for these Andes villagers.

Our trip was scheduled for about eight days in Peru, beginning and ending with a night in Lima. At the time the country was in chaos. Polio was running rampant down there, so we all got our shots before stepping foot on Peruvian soil. Also, we were landing in Peru just one week after the Falkland Islands invasion, so everything was on high alert. When we landed in Lima International Airport, guards armed to the hilt—with machine guns and ample ammunition draped over each shoulder—were everywhere. There was no conveyor belt to gently deliver our bags to us upon landing. Luggage was thrown unceremoniously out of the airplane and onto the runway. All of the bags were searched for weapons and/or drugs before being turned over to us with our shirts hanging out of the sides, the straps undone, and the locks pried open. We met the U.S. Ambassador that night, and he told cautionary tales of Americans rotting in Peruvian prisons on drug charges. The ambassador figured that an unreasonably large percentage of his job involved intervening on behalf of several wealthy American parents who were frantically trying to get their sons or daughters out of jail there. Even rich white Americans were generally unsuccessful in avoiding prison in Peru. The prison system there just snatched them up, threw them in, and forgot about them. The sentencing in Peru was inflexible—five years meant five years. To make matters worse, that was five years of hard labor with no human rights organizations on hand to make sure that they were treated humanely. The ambassador gave

I really enjoyed our visit to the Presidential Palace in Lima. **Photo courtesy of Elvin Bethea**

us further warning that it was not even safe for Americans to be on the streets of Lima after dark.

Our next stop in Lima was the President's Palace. The President of Peru and his wife were warm and gracious. The president could only meet with us very briefly because he was heading to Bolivia for some high level meetings about the Falklands. The first lady, however, was incredibly cordial and seemed genuinely interested in us and in the CARE project. The most impressive things to me on that presidential visit were the artifacts in the palace itself. There was a horse-drawn royal coach that looked like something out of "Cinderella." The palace was just filled with priceless artifacts and works of art that represented centuries of Peruvian culture. If I ever get my nerve up, I'd love to go back and see it all again. The armed guards, though, are a little intimidating.

Early the next morning we made our way to the mountains, and the drive took us along a beautiful coastline. I wasn't prepared for the fact that it was going to be a six-hour drive, however. We were traveling in two station wagons filled with Peruvian beer—a "healthy" alternative to the dysentery and other diseases that local water might bring upon us. The trek was difficult, and we didn't even make the first village on our itinerary that first day on the road, because the rains had washed out some roads on our way. At one point, the seven football players had to get out and lay down about eight or nine trees across a gap in the road so that we'd be able to get across. Despite the weather, the drive up the mountains themselves was pretty harrowing. There was barely enough room for one vehicle on the winding road and yet it was two-way traffic. We edged up very slowly, and as I looked over the side to my right, all I could see was dense forest. We were told some buses had gone off the edge in the past, and that just contributed to the whole white-knuckle experience of driving through the Andes.

Our first night was spent outdoors because we didn't make it to our first village. We parked the station wagons next to a field of coca leaf, and the project manager encouraged us to chew on one of the leaves to help with the lightheadedness from the altitude. He encouraged us to chew on coca whenever we needed it, but he warned us not to put any in our pockets or to try to take even a little bit home. As I heard his warning, visions of Peruvian prison danced in my head even though I was never remotely tempted to try to smuggle coca leaf back to the States. That night, a few of the guys slept in the station wagons, and the rest of us settled on the ground with our blankets, nestled on a bed of coca leaves. No matter where we were sleeping, everyone awoke at 2:30 a.m. to the rude rumblings of our first Peruvian earthquake. It was a memorable start to a memorable trip.

We arrived at the first village of our tour, right at a mountaintop. The villagers were colorful, beautiful, friendly people, and even though none of them knew what American football was, they seemed impressed by our size. We carried around football cards of ourselves and handed those out to the children, who were especially eager after our arrival. I would hand a card to one of the kids, and he would look at it, then look at me, then look at the card, and then back at me again. The look on his face was priceless as he began to grasp the whole concept.

The biggest thrill of the entire trip was playing soccer with the kids. Most of these villages had rocks on the ground everywhere, which made soccer difficult, but whatever they wanted, we did. Whatever it took to see those kids happy and laughing, we were committed to doing it.

That same evening, we were invited to dinner with a local family. As we walked into their home, I saw a big black pot, about four feet across and three feet deep. There was a fire blazing all around the pot and then I noticed the vegetables. Every one of them was cartoonishly super-sized, compared to the same vegeta-

The children of Peru were the most amazing part of the CARE trip.
Photo courtesy of Elvin Bethea

bles in the grocery stores back in the States. The potatoes were three times larger, the cabbages were the size of basketballs, the kernels of corn were multicolored and as big as marbles. I marveled at them when our guide turned to us.

"Just so you know, it is impolite to refuse to eat whatever they offer you," he whispered.

"Well, who could refuse those?" I thought as I stared at the incredible mega-vegetables.

My thought was interrupted by something that darted across the room. I looked down at the dirt floor and about 30 guinea pigs were running around the place. They were pets, but they apparently were also a meal. The villagers killed the poor varmints and then stuck a skewer through them that ran the length of their bodies. The guinea pigs were skinned, and then the skewers were stuck in the ground at an angle to cook over the fire. The skewer came out of their mouths, and each one still had his two little ears poking on each side of it. My fellow NFL ambassadors and I exchanged looks with each other that said, "Should we really eat this?" We all knew we had to do it. When in Peru, eat like the Peruvians. I remember nibbling daintily around the most unsavory parts of the guinea pig and trying to concentrate on the meatiest bits. I wish I could say that it tasted like chicken, but it didn't.

At the next village, we were greeted just as warmly as the last. We drank some local beer, and everyone seemed so delighted to see us. We mingled with the children, who were just as beautiful and charming as before, and we even played more soccer on even more rocks. While we were kicking the soccer ball around, we heard what sounded like Peruvian music, coming from a speaker!

"How did they ever get electricity all the way up here?" I asked myself, looking the small boxes.

It turns out the villagers were using an old car battery that they somehow had gotten, had hooked it up to their stereo, and had attached the speaker to a pole in the ground.

It was a joyous time. We hated to leave, but we had to stay on schedule and it was time to head for the next stop. I'll never forget one of the men in that village who was visibly upset that we were leaving. He wanted us to stay forever. We finally managed to reluctantly tear ourselves away from everyone, only to find that each of our station wagons had flat tires. Clearly, this man deflated them so we'd have to stay. Fortunately, there was a spare tire in each of the vehicles, or it's quite possible we'd still be in the Andes celebrating with that village, playing soccer, and eating more guinea pigs.

The next village on the itinerary was really more of a town. There was an open market where you could buy everything from local delicacies like goat's eye to special snakes for healing purposes. I bought a king-sized llama skin rug for about $50. There was even a motel of sorts in town, but it was several notches below a Motel 6. One of my most vivid memories was the full-hearted villager who pushed his way through the crowd to hug all of the football players. It wasn't until we finished hugging him that we noticed his coarse poncho was covered in burdocks and now we were, too. The children in these villages reminded me of my friends and myself in Trenton. They were all living in abject poverty, but they didn't seem to notice. They didn't know about anything else but their own life, so they just seemed incredibly happy with whom they were, what they had, and where they lived.

The holding tanks that we demonstrated in the various villages in the Andes seemed to be a big help to the Peruvian people. They were going to save labor and keep the villages much healthier. We arrived back in Lima with a feeling of great satisfaction and pride for the work we did in the mountains. The people in the capital had heard about us and wanted to meet the big American football players. Once again, the children in Lima wanted a soccer game with us. We passed through one of the most depressed, poverty-stricken neighborhoods of Lima and saw families living in cardboard huts. There were whole families sheltered in a tiny hovel that was pieced together with sections of cardboard boxes. Children were swimming and bathing in the same water supply used for drinking and cooking. It was the damnedest thing I'd ever seen. The city dump was cleared for our soccer game, and the smell was unlike anything I can describe. We had a great time with the kids, but we finally had to admit that we were pretty useless as soccer players. The kids had a lot of fun, and seeing those children so happy was the greatest experience of the entire trip.

The next day we returned to the Lima airport and the armed patrols, who were everywhere—on the city streets and at our hotel—seemed to be in full force. Our CARE representative cautioned us to stick close together, because the last thing he wanted was for us to get separated from the relative safety of our group while we were in the middle of this volatile airport.

At one point, I got a little distracted and noticed Benny Ricardo was over at a counter. I figured that we were boarding and Ricardo was leading the group onto our plane. As I headed over to the same counter with my passport in hand, Ricardo was led away. When I got to the counter, there was a bandolero, armed to the teeth, who glanced at my passport, barked something in Spanish to another guy, and then ordered me to go with the man. As I was led to a room down a corridor behind the counter, Ricardo came out of the room holding his belt and his shoes. I thought nothing of it as I walked in the door and found myself in a bathroom.

Inside the bathroom was a table, and the man instructed me to put my briefcase on the table and open it.

In Peru we passed out football cards with our photos on them to the people we met. **Photo courtesy of Elvin Bethea**

"Who am I to argue?" I thought as I looked at the man.

I did what I was told, and the official searched my briefcase. He found some chewing gum, put a stick of it in his mouth, and started chewing. By the look on his face, I can only assume he thought that I was part of an ingenious plot to smuggle coca leaves disguised as Wrigley's Spearmint Gum.

The search continued until he stumbled upon the football cards of myself that I had been handing out to the kids in the mountains.

"Is this you?" he asked suspiciously.

I nodded.

"What do you do for a living?"

"American football player," I said.

As soon as he heard my answer, the man leaned over to one of the stalls and started rattling off in high-speed Spanish.

"What is he doing?" I thought as I watched him speak to the stall door.

Then I realized someone had been in there the entire time.

My first interrogator slid the football cards under the stall and showed them to this new mystery man. He then turned to my llama skin rug, which was rolled and tied tightly with strong string. The string was cut, and the rug got patted down for signs of illegal packages. As I watched the interrogator examine my rug, I just happened to look out the window and see the airplane, which I was supposed to be on. The ramp to the plane was being taken away! That was a bad sign.

But I was trapped. I certainly couldn't say anything to the federales about hurrying along their investigation. As he continued the search and I watched the ramp get farther and farther away from the plane, I was getting mad as hell.

As quickly as I was whisked away, the search was over. The rug got rolled up, and I was released from custody. My only guess is that the football cards saved me.

I ran out the door to the plane, the stairs were returned, and I finally got on the plane. As soon as I was safely inside the airplane door, I started cussing out every one of my NFL brothers for almost taking off without me.

Shortly after we landed back on U.S. soil, I got off the plane, dropped to my knees, and kissed the ground. Everyone looked at me like I was crazy. The wonderful people of Peru were a great experience, and I'll always be proud of the difference we were able to make in the lives of those mountain villagers. I would do it all over again if CARE ever asked. It was just that I could go my whole lifetime without ever again experiencing that final scene in the bathroom of the Lima International Airport.

Chapter 9

THE LAST ROUND-UP

With apologies to Charles Dickens, I found 1982 to be the best of times and the worst of times. The best came in April when we went to Peru for CARE. The worst came as the 1982 season approached, and it became clearer with every passing day that a work stoppage was imminent. I had been the Oilers' player representative for the NFL Players Association since I took the job over from Kenny Houston in 1972, after Kenny was traded. Until 1982 came along, my work for the NFLPA had generally been interesting, occasionally rewarding, but mostly frustrating. In my 10th year as rep, however, it got downright ugly.

The NFLPA went on strike just before the third game of the 1982 season, and for the first time in league history, regular-season games were affected by players refusing to step onto the field.

We were fighting for the freedom that every other athlete in the major sports leagues enjoyed—free agency, the right to move on to another team when our option played itself out. We had begun demanding it as early as 1974, but it hadn't been until 1977 that we had signed a four-year agreement with NFL management. In 1981 when the four-year collective bargaining agreement between the union and management was about to expire, the talk of a strike had begun, because the owners were reluctant to renew the expired agreement. As it stood, if a player gambled by playing out his option, hoping for another contract, he ran the risk of getting a serious injury and losing all negotiating strength. There were plenty of players who refused to risk playing in the Pro Bowl, because getting hurt in your option year would drastically reduce your value. In order to express our opinion on this issue, the NFLPA had T-shirts made for the entire membership that graphically expressed our position. The T-shirt had an image of two burly arms shackled in chains with the words "No Freedom...No Football" emblazoned right above it.

During the strike negotiations the owners played a lot of mind games with us. They scheduled a meeting with us in New York City and then waited until we had our airline tickets booked, our hotel rooms reserved, and all of the arrangements in place. Then they cancelled the New York meeting and moved it to Miami at the last minute. They pulled a lot of chicken-shit pranks like that and relied on their tight-knit fraternity to hold together and keep up the collusion that they were using to hide their not-so-secret agenda. By sticking together, the owners were successfully keeping players' salaries down and secretly agreeing not to raid other teams for players whose options were running out.

Only a renegade such as Al Davis would defy this hidden agreement with his fellow owners. Subsequently, he signed some great veterans for his Raider teams, and they won a slew of Super Bowls in the process. Davis never seemed to have much use for the other owners, and by thumbing his nose at their collusion, he was also showing them that you've got to spend money to make money (and win championships). The owners never had much use for Davis either, but he proved that living well is the best revenge.

It was already tough enough to fight the owners, but it was doubly complicated when our own players worked against us, too. We expected to be undermined and punked by management during negotiations. In fact, whenever we met in New York, we always got rooms on the inside corridors of the hotel. If we met or stayed in rooms that faced other buildings too closely, we'd find that NFL spies or even sportswriters would be trying to pick up our conversations on boom mikes from nearby windows. However, I was naïve enough to assume that our fellow union brothers would not sell us out.

One morning I was awakened in New York by Gene Upshaw, the president of the NFLPA, and told that I needed to get back to Houston right away. He handed me a copy of the *Houston Chronicle* that announced several Oilers were on the verge of breaking the strike. I came home to Houston and found that middle linebacker Gregg Bingham and wide receiver Steve Bryant were getting together with some of the players to discuss returning to work.

Bingham and I had had our share of disagreements in the locker room, but I was just trying to bring Bingham back down to earth. He didn't like hearing "no" from anybody and certainly didn't like hearing other ways to do things on the field. It had to be his way or no way.

On the field Bingham had a tremendous heart and always seemed to be exactly where he had to be to make the play. He was so relentlessly effective that he still holds the all-time franchise record for tackles with 1,970. Bum Phillips said that to keep Bingham out of the game "you'd have to cut his head off and hide it." Bingham was a good, tough, smart linebacker and an integral part of our success as a team in the late 1970s. It was impossible not to appreciate a player with his brand of intensity and drive.

(I *really* admired his knack for always finding ways to make money. Since retiring from football, Bingham has done very well for himself with a chain of oil change outlets here in the Houston area. He was always a bona fide entrepreneur, but when I was mad at him, I called him an "entre-manure." One of his most ingenious money-making ideas is something that most people would not even have thought to do. Bingham amassed a very valuable coin collection by having someone sift through the coins that his customers put into the vending machines at his various businesses. Apparently, there's thousands and thousands of dollars in rare coins that people are unwittingly throwing away for a can of soda or a car wash. Who knew?!? Well, Gregg Bingham did, and it's made him a wealthy man.)

The strike had dragged on for about five weeks. During the first week everything had been fine, because there had been no big hardships for anybody and life seemed good. No one had been to training camp so everyone was fat, dumb, and happy. Then the weeks kept slipping by. By the third week, the money crunch had gotten serious for some guys, and by the next week, house payments had been due and several players had started to feel their buttholes tightening up. Along came the fifth week, and the wives were getting on their husbands' backs to go out and make some money.

I had always deferred a big portion of my contract money so that I had money coming in at all times, whether I was working or not. I had advised my fellow players to defer their money, too, especially when the strike seemed so likely to happen. Deferred money would have carried them through all of the games in a strike season. I had preached deferment to anybody who would listen, but most players hadn't done it. That was why all hell had broken loose.

Bingham and Bryant fed on our teammates' fears and panic. To settle everyone down, I got back to Houston to arrange a meeting to go over everything with my team. (If I could've found Bingham and Bryant before the meeting, I would have choked them. I never ran away from a good fight. Bum used to say we weren't going to win the game if I didn't get in a fight the week before.) I drove to that fateful meeting with my Oiler teammates behind the wheel of my brand new customized $20,000 van. It was called "The Love Van" because it had a heart-shaped window in the back, along with liquor dispensers, roll-down seats, and plush burgundy upholstery. If I drove up in that van today, it would be called a pimped-out ride.

Well, my teammates were convinced I had sold them out to the owners and got some kind of kickback to buy the van. They were angry, and they wanted answers.

"I told you guys to defer your money," I explained very calmly. "Old money bought this van, not new money."

I spent the rest of the meeting begging my own teammates to stick together with our union and me. We had to show a united front to the owners and the league if we were going to win this fight. They finally agreed to stay on strike, but there was a lot of blood on the carpet by the end of that meeting. It was an unpleasantly eye-opening experience.

The strike ended in mid-November when the NFLPA signed a new collective bargaining agreement that ran through 1986. (Four years after I retired from the NFL, the players had another strike in 1987 when their demands for free agency still went unmet. Ultimately, it finally took the U.S. District Court in Minneapolis to bring free agency to the league. The federal court ruled on behalf of the players and proclaimed that the league was in violation of antitrust laws for not allowing unrestricted movement of players.)

During that year I was also able to get our Pro Bowl money increased. We had been getting $1,500 each for the winners and $750 each for the losers on the Pro Bowl teams. Our efforts raised the money to $5,000 and $2,500, respectively.

The things we couldn't achieve for our union membership were the sadder parts of my job. We were fighting for players like Darryl Stingley, who had been a quadraplegic ever since a catastrophic injury during a game and was only getting $3,000 a month from the NFL. We ended up fighting for the players who are in the league today and who reap the benefits of all of our hard work on the frontlines of labor negotiations. The average NFL punter now earns more in a season than I got for my last five seasons combined. The league minimum, which is paid to anyone who does so much as sit on the bench waiting to do a long snap, is actually more than my highest year's salary. The scars are still there from those battles between the union and management in the 1970s and 1980s. There was a cooling-off period after the strikes, but the embers are still burning 20 years later. The owners enjoyed those bitter fights, because more often than not they drove a wedge between our own union brothers. I'm a living example of that wedge. I was a bad guy to the owners, but they couldn't get rid of me, and I was a bad guy to some of the players.

After signing that last NFLPA agreement with management in 1982, I resigned as the Oilers' player rep. I got home, gathered up everything I owned with the NFLPA logo on it, and carried the stuff into the backyard. I put everything—T-shirts, papers, correspondence, brochures—into a metal tub and covered the contents with gasoline. Then I dropped in a lighted match and watched it burn. I had been fighting owners, and even my fellow players, for more than 10 years. Now my goal was to avoid hearing the letters *NFLPA* ever again.

After we went back to work, the Oilers finished at 1-8 in the strike-shortened 1982 season, and I was ready to hang up the cleats.

In the home stretch of any long career in professional sports, it is difficult for an athlete not to reflect back. Actually, it is probably impossible not to reflect back, and after 14 years in the NFL, 1982 was a tough season for so many reasons. There was the strike, of course, but there was also the toll on my body. After all those years in the trenches, it just got harder and harder during the offseason to get up for a work out and a long run in the morning. The mental preparation was getting tougher and my body was screaming, "Hey!" at me during every sprint.

I always set a goal for myself before every season. I wasn't motivated by fame or glory or even money. I could've played in front of an empty stadium, if necessary (as an Oiler, in fact, it was often necessary). I always had something to prove to myself every season. I felt I had to be the best defensive end in the league because guys like Jack Youngblood, Deacon Jones, and L.C. Greenwood all got better press in their cities than I did in Houston. I always tried to be better by one or two tackles, or one or two sacks, every season. I took film home with me all of the time. I needed to see my offensive tackle matchup for the coming week, so I watched their previous two games. I watched Doug Dieken, I watched Jon Kolb, I watched John Hannah, I watched Leon Gray, Anthony Munoz, Art Shell, Jim Tyrer, and so on, and so on. I was looking for their weaknesses and strengths, and I'm sure they were doing the same thing with me. In practices, I'd get one of my teammates to play the role of a particular opposing tackle and test me out on some of the tricks they'd be using in the next game. I'd always do the same for them with their defensive end matchup, too. Setting goals in those final two seasons was an exercise in futility, because there just wasn't much gas left in my tank.

Too many players think they're going to last longer than the game. They don't think about the younger, faster players who are coming into the league. They don't think about career-ending injuries. They think that they'll decide when the game is over for them, but very few of us have that luxury. (Personally, I could've done without the 1982 and 1983 seasons, where the Oilers amassed a combined record of 3-22. Ouch.)

Coach Biles tried to talk me into staying for one more season. He said I could serve as a mentor/unofficial coach to some of the younger players, and that appealed to me, but I was still fairly determined to end the ride. I just wasn't sure that I had the mental and physical strength to leave it all on the field for another season. I had been working with Anheuser-Busch in the off-season since 1978, and I was ready to make the transition to a life away from football. Word got around that I was about to call it quits in the NFL, and Bob Allen, one of Houston's most venerable television sports directors, did a full segment on my retirement for one of his broadcasts.

I had known since 1979 that I'd never see another AFC championship game, so what was the point in hanging around after my prime? I was getting older, the team was breaking up and new faces were coming in. The wave had been ridden and was now crashing on the beach. I was perfectly content to ride off into the sunset.

As a formality, I was called into Lad Herzeg's office to discuss a contract for 1983. I was in the driver's seat, because I didn't even want to come back, and that meant I could ask for almost anything. Because I wasn't planning to return, and I knew they'd never agree to an enormous raise, I decided to ask for my biggest payday ever. I demanded $300,000 for the 1983 season. Herzeg and his front office brass sputtered a bit, but then they politely dismissed me with the promise that they would think about it. I knew that I had just successfully priced myself out of any more badgering from the Oilers to come back for the 1983 season.

I was wrong.

A week later the phone rang. It was Coach Biles.

"When are you coming in to sign the papers?" he asked. "You've got your $300,000."

"Damn," I thought, "I should have asked for $500,000."

The first day of practice for the 1983 season was a bitch. Those young kids had me running all over the field, and I was pooped. When I got back into the locker room after that first day, I saw an article written by Ed Fowler of the *Houston Post* posted on the board. It was negative, as usual. I'd never seen nor heard of Fowler writing a positive article about anyone, so it came as no surprise, but this was the worst possible day for me to see something like that in print. As I walked through the locker room, I saw Fowler standing there, looking for someone to talk to. I zeroed in on him and confronted him about the article. As I laid into him, I just got madder and madder. The madder I got, the closer to Fowler I got. Guys were trying to pull me back, but we were now nose to nose.

"Don't hit him!" someone yelled as the argument reached its peak.

"I can't hit him," I thought, "but I can spit on him."

I stared straight into his eyes and just spit in his face.

He just stood there and took it like a man. It was not my proudest moment, and even if I didn't believe it before, that incident just confirmed for me that I didn't want to be in any more training camps. It was bad enough to go through 1-13 seasons without dealing with endlessly negative media types like Fowler who brought out the worst in me.

There was a big bright spot for me in the 1982 and 1983 seasons. My last two years in the league were also the first two years for a supernaturally gifted offensive lineman out of Penn State named Mike Munchak. Munchak and I had plenty of scuffles during practices, and he was a tough opponent. I admired the fact that this young rookie kid wouldn't back down from a 16-year veteran. It was easy to see that Munchak would be something special. He was a trench fighter, a real smashmouth football player. His technique was unbelievable. He had incredible balance and agility, coupled with superhuman strength—the whole package—as an offensive lineman. The offensive line tandem of Mike Munchak and Bruce Matthews (who joined the Oilers as a rookie in 1983) became a legendary one that is right up there with John Hannah and Leon Gray on the Patriots. Munchak was inducted in the Pro Football Hall of Fame in 2001, and it's inevitable that Matthews will join us in the Hall as soon as he's eligible.

Coach Biles's head-coaching tenure with the Oilers ended after the sixth game of the 1983 season. We were 0-6. Coach Biles was replaced by his defensive coordinator, Chuck Studley. I

December 11, 1983. This ceremony was held after I played my final game in the Astrodome. We beat Cleveland 34-27. **Lou Witt/Titans**

My good friend and favorite quarterback Dan Pastorini goes for some laughs at my retirement dinner. **Titans**

didn't like Coach Studley from the first day I laid eyes on him. He gave me the impression that he thought he knew everything, and I didn't respect him or anything he did. Without mincing words, I thought he was an asshole and an all-around weasel. Under his "leadership," we limped to a 2-8 finish for the last 10 games. I ended my final season in the NFL with a record of 2-14. As Yogi Berra would say, "It was déjà vu all over again."

I honestly don't regret staying to play for that last year, in spite of Coach Studley. Perhaps my only regret about that last season, besides our abysmal record, was the fact that I didn't get much playing time. It may seem like a contradiction that I didn't even want to play that last season, but I still complained about a lack of playing time. It's just this—if I'm going to be on the team, then I want to play as much as possible. So I suppose my playing career ended not with a bang, but a whimper. When I finally retired after the 1983 season, I had a little over $1 million in deferred money to be paid out over the next 10 years. I also had my job with Anheuser-Busch for another $30,000 per year. Two divorces and some bad investments put a crimp in some of that gravy, but I was looking forward to a happy retirement. How could I have predicted that some of the very best was yet to come?

Chapter 10

MY SMASHMOUTH HALL OF FAME

Except for the little matter of our meager salaries, I don't think there was a better time to play in the NFL than the 1970s. The abundance of outstanding talent and colorful personalities made it lots of fun to go to work, even if it meant getting your ass kicked on a regular basis. I got to experience the end of the AFL era and then the historic merger with the NFL. I got to marvel at the incredible dynasties and football juggernauts created in Dallas, Miami, and Pittsburgh. I got to test myself, week in and week out, against some of the greatest players in the history of the league. It almost made it worth the lousy money just to have the opportunity to be around players like these.

Please don't think I'm taking anything away from the hard-nosed, tough-as-nails, smashmouth football players of the 1920s, 1930s, 1940s, 1950s, and 1960s. Names such as Red Grange, "Bronko" Nagurski, Benny Friedman, Fritz Pollard, Johnny "Blood" McNally, Jim Thorpe, "Bulldog" Turner, Sammy Baugh, Sid Luckman, "Ace" Parker, "Bullet Bill" Dudley, Charley Trippi, Pete Pihos, Marion Motley, Bill Willis, Tony Canadeo, George Musso, AlexWojciechowicz, Otto Graham, Steve Van Buren, Bobby Layne, Dick "Night Train" Lane, Jack Christiansen, Yale Lary, Emlen Tunnell, Artie Donovan, Jim Parker, Joe Perry, Ernie Stautner, Norm Van Brocklin, Doak Walker, Chuck Bednarik, Bob St. Clair, Lou Creekmur, Hugh McElhenny, Andy Robustelli, Y.A.Tittle, Jim Brown, Gino Marchetti, Joe Schmidt, Johnny Unitas, Lou Groza, Rosie Brown, Jim Taylor , Len Ford, Leo Nomellini, Bart Starr, Bill George, Henry Jordan, Forrest Gregg, Jim Ringo, Sam Huff, Mike McCormack, Frank Gatski, Stan Jones, and so many more were the gold standard for smashmouth football. These guys are all of my teammates in the Pro Football Hall of Fame now, but I deeply regret never getting the chance to play against these legendary names from the first five decades of pro football. If you don't recognize some of these men, do yourself a favor and look them up.

The players in the NFL today are getting bigger than ever, faster than ever, and richer than ever. Better than ever? That's debatable. The imposition of stiff fines and suspensions have legislated smashmouth football out of existence. Eye gouging, leg whips, pile drivers, and clothesline tackles are the sole property of professional wrestling now. It's all staged when you see those maneuvers on Wrestlemania, but back in the day during a game in the NFL, you never knew when it was coming. If Doug Dieken, my favorite nemesis on any opposing offensive line, tried to engage in one of our classic street fights during a pro game right now, we'd each be fined $25,000 in the first quarter, then fined another $50,000 in the second quarter, and before the third quarter was over, we'd each have five-game suspensions. Call me crazy, but I miss those days.

So to pay tribute to some of the exceptional gladiators with whom I did battle in the football arena from 1968 to 1983, I've created my own Smashmouth Hall of Fame. The only limitation I've placed on myself is to keep it to the guys against whom I actually played. So there are no defensive players here. This Hall of Fame is only quarterbacks, running backs, offensive linemen, and special teams, plus a pair of head coaches for good measure. Drum roll, please. Here's Elvin Bethea's Smashmouth Hall of Fame:

The Quarterbacks

Ken Anderson
Cincinnati Bengals, 1971-1986

College: Augustana (Illinois)
Pro Bowls: 1976, 1977, 1982, 1983
Honors: 1981 NFL MVP

Anderson was a deadly accurate passer and a physically tough competitor. He was a double threat, because he could slice you to ribbons with those pinpoint laser receptions, or he could just run at you if he ever got stuck without an open receiver. Anderson really knew how to move the ball around.

I remember a game against the Bengals in 1975 that showed me just how dangerous he could be. Curley Culp and I were zoning in on Anderson from either side of him. We had him in our sights, and we both moved in for the kill. I just knew I was going to get him and, apparently, so did Culp. Just as Culp and I closed in and made our final commitment to the tackle, Anderson moved forward to avoid us. From that moment, until about 30 minutes later, I was out cold. Culp and I had made serious contact with each other's heads. Maybe I wasn't totally unconscious, but all of my senses and my feelings in the extremities were gone. I lay on the turf of a nationally televised game for almost half an hour. There were people standing around me asking if I was okay, but I couldn't move a thing. Yes, Kenny Anderson was a tough, smart competitor with great instincts. We lost that game 21-19.

TERRY BRADSHAW
Pittsburgh Steelers, 1970-1983

College: Louisiana Tech
Pro Bowls: 1976, 1979,1980
Honors: Super Bowl XIII MVP; Super Bowl XIV MVP;
Pro Football Hall of Fame, Class of 1989

In Bradshaw's first regular-season game as a pro, he played the Oilers in Pittsburgh and we beat him 19-7. Well, I shouldn't say we beat him, because he was taken out of the game in the third quarter after only completing four passes on 16 attempts. We heard later that he cried in the parking lot after the game. From that inauspicious debut, Bradshaw used his incredible mental toughness (no quarterback has probably ever had to take more criticism from his own team, coaches, fans, and reporters) and impressive physical toughness (he broke ribs, wrists, and who knows what else?) to shape himself into one of the greatest champions in NFL history.

Bradshaw seemed as big as we were on the defensive line. He had remarkable running skills, and that always makes it difficult for the defensive line to cover a quarterback. When Bradshaw started running consistently in a game, we knew we were in for a long day. As long as he was on the field, he was going to be a threat to hurt the defense somehow, so we always tried to knock him out of the game. The mistaken reputations he had for immaturity and poor leadership skills were probably fine for someone to say if they hadn't played against him. Once you had to face him on the field, however, you knew you were up against an outstanding quarterback who was never better than when the game was a big one. There isn't another quarterback I've seen who I'd rather have on my side if I absolutely, positively *had* to win the game.

LEN DAWSON
Kansas City Chiefs, 1962-1975

College: Purdue
Pro Bowls: 1963, 1965.1967, 1968, 1969, 1970, 1972
Honors: 1962 AFL MVP; Super Bowl IV MVP;
Pro Football Hall of Fame, Class of 1987

Dawson was another amazingly accurate passer who also added the dimension of cucumber coolness and poise under pressure. We knew he was going to stay in the pocket and was not a big threat to run, but the key was trying to get around his offensive line. Guys such as Jim Tyrer and Ed Budde were big as houses and very intimidating obstacles. Dawson was another smart quarterback, and he was very quick in getting the ball released. Whatever you brought at him, he knew how to manage it and seemed to get it all done without even dirtying his uniform (that's how he earned the nickname "Ajax").

Dawson was an excellent field general, so your only chance of getting somewhere with him was to force his hand and try to pressure him into a hasty decision. Believe me, it sounds easier than it was, and that's why Len Dawson is right where he belongs—in the Hall of Fame.

♦ ♦ ♦ ♦ ♦

DAN FOUTS
San Diego Chargers, 1973-1987

College: Oregon
Pro Bowls: 1980, 1981, 1982, 1983, 1984, 1986
Honors: 1982 NFL MVP;
Pro Football Hall of Fame, Class of 1993

Fouts's career took off when Don Coryell arrived in San Diego to take over head-coaching duties in 1978. Fouts put the "air" into "Air Coryell." By conservative estimate, I'd say Fouts threw about four million passes each game and completed about 60 percent of them. Or at least it seemed that way. Fouts had tremendous skills and great brains. He was a little cocky, but he had a right to be. To a lowly defensive lineman like me, he seemed untouchable.

The press would build up players like Fouts, and when we got a hold of some of the press clippings in the week before a game, we'd have dramatic readings in the Oiler locker room. It would get us charged up. You see, part of the real fun of the game of football is to go out and show the world that you're better than everyone thought you were. This was especially satisfying for those of us on teams like the Houston Oilers, because no one was expecting anything from us!

As great a player as Fouts was, I had my greatest game against him. It was in the 1978 playoffs, and he had just finished a season where he threw for about 87 million yards (okay, only 3,000 yards, but who's counting?). We went into that playoff game battered and bruised and minus a few key offensive weapons, like Dan Pastorini and Kenny Burrough. We had something to prove that day, and prove it we did. Fouts threw seven interceptions, including four to Vernon Perry alone. I sacked Fouts four times and recovered a fumble.

That particular game does not take anything away from the greatness of Dan Fouts's incredible Hall of Fame career, but it does illustrate how a defense that has something to prove can be deadlier than an offense that doesn't.

BOB GRIESE
Miami Dolphins, 1967-1980

College: Purdue
Pro Bowls: 1968, 1969, 1971, 1972,
1974, 1975, 1978, 1979
Honors: 1971 NFL MVP;
Pro Football Hall of Fame, Class of 1990

The Dolphins ran a ball-control offense with a tremendously efficient running attack. Those championship Miami teams in the 1970s were a genuine football dynasty, and they were led on the field by the poised, studious, intellectual Bob Griese. If you gave Griese the opportunity, he'd be quite able and willing to put up as many points on the board as the game clock would allow.

Griese wasn't just a great mind, though, he was also a helluva leader with a helluva supporting cast on the offense—Larry Csonka, Mercury Morris, Jim Kiick, Larry Little, Jim Langer, Bob Kuechenberg, Paul Warfield, and Earl Morrall, to name a few. A team like that could finish you off without breaking a sweat, and our motivation for getting hyped up for a game against the Dolphins was based on the desire to minimize any potential embarrassment. Needless to say, like a good many other teams in 1972, we were one of Miami's casualties in their perfect 17-0 season. Don't let his glasses fool you—Griese may have looked like a college professor, but he was a first-class Hall of Fame quarterback.

JOHN HADL
Teams: San Diego Chargers, 1962-1972;
L.A. Rams, 1973-1974;
Green Bay Packers, 1974-1975;
Houston Oilers, 1976-1977

College: Kansas
Pro Bowls: 1965, 1966, 1969, 1970, 1973, 1974

I played against John Hadl, I played with John Hadl, and I liked him a lot. Hadl always smiled. You'd knock him down with your best shot, and then he'd hop to his feet with a big, open smile on his face as if to say, "I'm still here. You didn't hit me *that* hard!"

Naturally, I thought I'd had a great lick on him, so the psychological advantage went to Hadl every time he pulled that. I admire that kind of gamesmanship.

His arm was strong and accurate, and I genuinely thought he was a very talented quarterback. As a person, though, I liked Hadl even more—he was down to earth and not even remotely cocky. When you can combine smashmouth skills with humility and earthiness, then you definitely belong in *my* Hall of Fame.

ARCHIE MANNING
New Orleans Saints, 1971-1982;
Houston Oilers, 1982-1983

College: Ole Miss
Pro Bowls: 1979, 1980
Honors: 1978 NFC MVP

Manning was another quarterback whom I knew both as opponent and teammate. As a Saint, I used to beat up on

Manning all of the time, but that certainly wasn't any fault of his. He was a Hall of Fame player stuck on a Hall of Shame team. His offensive line just could not protect him. Back when they used to have the goalposts right on the first line of the end zone, I drove poor Manning right into one of those in a game. Hey, the Oilers were certainly bad for years at a time, but the Saints were even worse and for a longer period of time, and I felt badly for the predicament that Manning had for himself.

On the field, Manning could scramble when he had to, and he had to on a regular basis. If the Saints were facing third and 20 and Manning had a chance to break out for a run, they'd be looking at first and 10 before you knew it.

As great as he was as a player, Archie Manning is an even greater person. He's a class act. When his son Peyton was playing in the 2003 Pro Bowl in Hawaii, I was there for my first official public appearance with my fellow inductees of the Pro Football Hall of Fame Class of 2003. Peyton made a special point to come over and congratulate me on behalf of the Manning family, which really impressed me as a typically first-class gesture. The acorn doesn't fall too far from the tree, as they say. If he had played almost anywhere else in the league, there's no doubt in my mind that Archie Manning would in the Pro Football Hall of Fame already. For now, he'll have to settle for Elvin's Smashmouth Hall of Fame.

JOE NAMATH
New York Jets, 1965-1976;
Los Angeles Rams, 1977

College: Alabama
Pro Bowls: 1966, 1968, 1969, 1970, 1973
Honors: 1968 AFL MVP; Super Bowl III MVP;
All-Time AFL Team; Pro Football Hall of Fame, Class of 1985

When I first came into the AFL in 1968, Namath was already a legend. He was the first player to get a $400,000 contract and the first quarterback to throw for 4,000 yards in a season. He gave legitimacy to the AFL with his guarantee that his upstart Jets would defeat the venerable Baltimore Colts in Super Bowl III—and then he did it! He was exciting, glamorous, and enormously popular, and he made the cover of every magazine, thanks to his status as the most eligible swinging bachelor in the country. Listen, I would have been happy to touch the hem of his garment, much less tackle him.

With his white shoes and the long, flowing hair coming out of the back of his helmet, Namath had a style and a flair that no one in the league had then or has ever had since. I felt like I really accomplished something if I could get my hands on him just once or twice in a game. Between his golden arm, his sharp mind, and his one-of-a-kind elegance (not to mention a top-notch receiving corps), a team like the Oilers always felt like we were entering into a lopsided situation for every game with the New York Jets. We just felt lucky to keep it close. We knew Namath couldn't run because of his cursed knees. He ran like he was carrying a 100-pound sack of cement on his back. Nevertheless, even when he wasn't always good, he was never dull. More than 30 years later, I still feel that just being able to say that I played on the same field as Joe Namath was really the cream in my coffee.

BRIAN SIPE
Cleveland Browns, 1974-1983

College: San Diego State
Pro Bowl: 1981

Don't let the relative lack of honors fool you, Brian Sipe was a real warrior who could beat any defense in the league. When the great quarterbacks of the 1970s are being discussed, Sipe doesn't get much mention for some reason. He took some lickings from me, to be sure. I recently saw some film of a game we played against the Browns and there was a play where I got to him, lifted him off the ground, and drove his head right into the turf. If I did that in a game today, I'd be fined the equivalent of my entire 1975 season's salary! Sipe, however, just got up after the hit and kept right on playing. Now, *that's* smashmouth! Sipe was also a great guy off the field, and we had some great games against his Browns in 1970s.

ROGER STAUBACH
Dallas Cowboys, 1969-1979

College: Navy
Pro Bowls: 1972, 1976, 1977, 1978, 1979, 1980
Honors: 1963 Heisman Trophy; Super Bowl VI MVP;
Pro Football Hall of Fame, Class of 1985

"Captain Comeback" came to the NFL as a 27-year-old rookie in 1969, after serving his four years of active duty in Vietnam. He arrived as sort of the anti-Namath. Namath was a free-wheeling, high-living, good-time guy with a reputation for supernatural success with the ladies, and Roger Staubach was the rock-solid, milk-drinking, All-American boy.

On the field, Staubach's Cowboys were a fearsome bunch that required every opponent to bring their best possible game. You couldn't just bring 100 percent, or even the mythical 110 percent. You'd better have 150 percent! Staubach could run, and he had this quick move that would punish any defense that made the mistake of going inside on him. If you went inside on Staubach, he'd make that little move and bring the ball down, then he'd run right for the spot you just left. Before you knew it, he was past you, and it was first down, Dallas Cowboys, and you were just another notch on their belt as they headed for another NFC championship and another Super Bowl.

Getting a good lead on Staubach was never enough to help you relax, because if there was time on the clock, he'd find a way to catch up and then win. Staubach was book smart and football smart, and he could do anything in the game. When Dallas finally got the chance to have Staubach's brains and talent standing behind that awesome Cowboy offensive line, it spelled doom and misery for any opposing team.

FRAN TARKENTON
New York Giants, 1967-1971;
Minnesota Vikings, 1972-1978

College: Georgia
Pro Bowls: 1968, 1969, 1970, 1971, 1975, 1976, 1977
Honors: Pro Football Hall of Fame, Class of 1986

Just when you thought you had your hands on this little guy, you didn't. You just never got a clean shot at him. The Vikings had a great offensive line, including names such as Mick

Tingelhoff and Ron Yary, so if you ever *did* get a crack at bringing Tarkenton down, it meant there had to have been some breakdown in that line. So let's assume that all of the planets aligned in just the perfect way and I was now back there with a chance to take Tarkenton down for a sack—how do I catch him?!? Whenever you made a great move for him or took a world-class dive to bring him down, Tarkenton would be gone by the time you got there. This guy was quick *and* fast. Fran Tarkenton was the first white boy I ever saw with real speed. Hey, I was fast, but Tarkenton could outrun me.

The Running Backs

EMERSON BOOZER
New York Jets, 1966-1975

College: Maryland East Shore
Pro Bowls: 1967, 1969

Boozer and I were supposed to have played on the same college team. But because I ended up at North Carolina A&T, instead of Maryland East Shore, we played against each other for two years in college and then again in the pros. Boozer was a classy back, but he loved to talk smack. He was a helluva running back, and once he got past the first wave on the defensive line, the secondary had best get their straps on, because it was game on. With a name like Emerson Boozer, you just *knew* something bad would happen if you got in his way when he was on a run.

LARRY CSONKA
Miami Dolphins, 1968-1974, 1979;
New York Giants, 1976-1978

College: Syracuse
Pro Bowls: 1971, 1972, 1973, 1974, 1975
Honors: Super Bowl VIII MVP;
Pro Football Hall of Fame, Class of 1987

Larry Csonka was a big, tough white boy. At six foot three and 240 pounds, he was just about as big as the defensive linemen he was smashing into game in and game out. Csonka would muscle out yards like a classic bulldozing fullback, and when you got a hold of him during a run, you might as well be grabbing a Brahma bull.

First of all, you had to get past that Miami offensive line (Larry Little, Jim Langer, Bob Kuechenberg, etc.) and then you had to get past Jim Kiick as the lead blocker in the backfield. If you weren't prepared for the hit that was coming from Csonka when he lowered his shoulder and barreled into you, it was lights out. Csonka could do damage. Then, to top it all off, he only fumbled once for every 100 carries, on average. It hardly seems fair, does it?

FRANCO HARRIS
Pittsburgh Steelers, 1972-1983;
Seattle Seahawks, 1984

College: Penn State
Pro Bowls: 1973, 1974, 1975, 1976,
1977, 1978, 1979, 1980, 1981
Honors: Super Bowl IX MVP;
Pro Football Hall of Fame, Class of 1990

Harris capped his phenomenal rookie year in 1972 with an obscure little catch against the Raiders in the AFC playoffs. It was a deflected pass called "The Immaculate Reception," and it propelled the Steelers to their first playoff victory. Maybe you've heard of it?

When Harris started to beat you in a game, you had to run as fast as you could to the sidelines because that's where he was headed. If he ran up into the stands, we were going to follow him. We called him "East-West Franco" because that's the direction he'd be running—east and west toward the sidelines. I don't blame him. It showed some real brains. He'd only blast you head-on when it was essential to get the yardage. If the yardage was gravy or the Steelers had a big lead, he'd run out of bounds and save his body for another battle.

Harris wasn't a deadly power back, but he could outmaneuver you with his quickness in getting on the outside. He was deceiving and could really do anything you wanted a back to do—run, catch, block. At some point in every game, one of his socks would roll down because he couldn't get it over his knee. When you saw Harris's sock down, you knew it was going to be a long day to try to stop him.

◆ ◆ ◆ ◆ ◆

LEROY KELLY
Cleveland Browns, 1964-1973

College: Morgan State
Pro Bowls: 1967, 1968, 1969, 1970, 1971, 1972
Honors: Pro Football Hall of Fame, Class of 1994

Kelly was my man. He still is, really. There was just something about Kelly, even to this day, that you just have to respect. He played under the tutelage of Jim Brown, so to no one's surprise, Kelly inherited Brown's classiness as a back.

The two things that made Kelly especially dangerous were his deceptive speed and the fact that he would try to punish the tackler. He just put that huge shoulder down, and he'd try to take you down. If you stood there waiting for him, he'd already have five yards before you knew it. So if you wanted to make a dent in the Cleveland running game, you had to take it to him.

Game films are a good way to prepare for an opposing player's signature moves, but the films don't always tell the whole story. On the films, Kelly didn't look as quick as he really was when you were on the field with him. There was just no way to prepare for a back who looked slower on film than he was in a game. One second he would be right there, and the next second he was somewhere over there. Despite his brilliant running career in the NFL, Leroy Kelly was eligible for Hall of Fame induction for 15 years before finally making it. I'd love to hear someone try to explain how that could possibly happen.

GREG PRUITT
Cleveland Browns, 1973-1981,
Los Angeles Raiders, 1982-1984

College: Oklahoma
Pro Bowls: 1975, 1975, 1977, 1978, 1984

When Greg Pruitt played, all you could see was teeth, because he always smiled. If he ran one back on you, he smiled. If he scored a touchdown, he smiled. If you knocked him down behind the line of scrimmage for a three-yard loss, he smiled. Hell, why shouldn't he smile? He could do everything.

The Cleveland Browns were in our division, and when we saw their game films to prepare for them twice a year, we knew we had to stop Pruitt to win. He was a back who could do surprising, unexpected things to muck up the defense. He was fast *and* he had moves, which is not something you can say about every running back. He was a kick returner, too, and almost the equal of Billy "White Shoes" Johnson. So when a player does that many things to help his team *and* does it with a smile—he's a definite Smashmouth Hall of Famer.

O.J. SIMPSON
Buffalo Bills, 1969-1977,
San Francisco 49ers, 1978-1979

College: USC
Pro Bowls: 1970, 1973, 1974, 1975, 1976, 1977
Honors: 1968 Heisman Trophy; 1972, 1973, 1975 NFL MVP;
NFL 75th Anniversary Team;
Pro Football Hall of Fame, Class of 1985

Simpson came to the AFL as another big-dollar guy, and he definitely gave everyone the impression that we were supposed to look up to him. Well, we *did* look up to him—until we got on the field.

The Oilers tended to over-prepare for every game against Simpson and his Bills because he embarrassed every team that Buffalo played against. Running behind the brilliant blocking of his "Electric Company" (Joe DeLamielleure and Reggie McKenzie), Simpson steamrolled right over every team in the league, especially in 1973, when he ran for a record-breaking 2,003 yards. Simpson ran for big yardage against every team in 1973—*except* the Houston Oilers. He even wrote in his autobiography that the one team that gave him no ground that season was the Oilers. Simpson also wrote that the Astrodome was the worst turf he ever played on, and that the Bills' 1973 game there was the worst beating he had ever gotten. The pleasure was all ours, O.J.!

I got to know "The Juice" at the Pro Bowl every year. He was always a great guy to hang around with, because we knew that's where the women would be. Wherever Simpson went, women were sure to follow. Any women whom Simpson rejected were good enough for us!

We were always friends off the field, but we were very different. Simpson was "Hollywood," and I was Trenton. Guys like me just stood in the glow of his reflected glory and hoped to get in a picture with him that might make the papers. (A little publicity can never hurt at contract time.) Later, when you'd see your picture in the paper with Simpson, it somehow appeared that you were standing two feet behind him. How did he do that?

During a game, whenever he got tackled hard, Simpson never pissed and moaned about it like a lot of prima donnas. He'd just pick himself up and get back to it. As a running back, he was just mystifying. His skills were amazing. He made runs that were as beautiful as any ballet. There are some old-timers who will tell you that Red Grange was the best runner ever. There's also the legendary Jim Brown to consider, and certainly Gale Sayers has to get some votes, too. I played against O.J. Simpson at his peak, and even though he never ran for more than 55 yards against our Oiler defense, it's difficult to imagine that there could be too many backs who were ever better.

Tight Ends

DAVE CASPER
Oakland Raiders, 1974-1980; Houston Oilers, 1980-1983; Minnesota Vikings, 1983; Los Angeles Raiders, 1984

College: Notre Dame
Pro Bowls: 1977, 1978, 1979, 1980, 1981
Honors: Pro Football Hall of Fame, Class of 2001

As a Raider, Dave "The Ghost" Casper was one of my opponents at tight end for several years, but he also became one of my Oiler teammates in 1980. Until I got to practice against him in

Houston, I had never imagined that this curly-headed blond kid from California could do such amazing things as a blocker.

Casper was big enough to be a defensive lineman (about six foot four, 235 pounds), but he could twist his arms and his body in a way that gave me so much trouble when we faced each other. He was a nut case off the field, and I mean that in a good way, but on the field, Dave Casper was *serious*. He made opposing defensive linemen beat him in a game, but even if we did beat him, he'd still keep coming. Casper never wore protection on his arms, so the AstroTurf would burn off his skin regularly. Nevertheless, he'd just keep going back for more. I always admired that kind of toughness. It was smashmouth. After waiting for much too long, Dave Casper finally ended up right where he belongs—in the Pro Football Hall of Fame.

RAY CHESTER
Oakland Raiders, 1970-1972, 1978-1981; Baltimore Colts, 1973-1977

College: Morgan State
Pro Bowls: 1971, 1972, 1973, 1980

I was always telling Chester to stop holding me during the game. Chester just put up his hands with a wounded look on his face.

"I'm not holding!" he said very innocently. "Ask the referee! I'm not holding!"

Chester just constantly got in my way and tried to piss me off to get me off of my game. You have to respect any tight end who can do that to a defensive lineman. He didn't have the killer instinct, but he always got in my way enough to give his offence that extra second or two to get things rolling for them. Ray Chester was a finesse player.

JOHN MACKEY
Baltimore Colts, 1963-1971,
San Diego Chargers, 1972

College: Syracuse
Pro Bowls: 1964, 1966, 1967, 1968, 1969
Honors: NFL 75th Anniversary Team;
Pro Football Hall of Fame, Class of 1992

Mackey was the second tight end ever inducted into the Pro Football Hall of Fame. When Mike Ditka was making his acceptance speech as the first tight end to get inducted, he showed a lot of class and humility by admitting that Mackey should have had that honor before him. Ditka was right. Mackey was the prototype for a great tight end—he could overpower you with his tremendous blocking skills, he could catch anything that was thrown to him, and he had the kind of breakaway speed that could burn you for a touchdown on any given play.

Mackey was a man's man. He was a classy guy and a monumental human being in every respect. I'm only using the past tense, because now that he is in the throes of a dementia that strongly resembles Alzheimer's, he is no longer the John Mackey that I knew. When I saw him again at my Hall of Fame induction after so many years, I didn't recognize him. I was in total shock. I didn't know who he was. This illness has ravaged him to the point that he really only repeats the same four or five sentences. Because he's not able to reminisce with us about those great times on the football field, all we can do is clutch onto a few vivid memories of the John Mackey that we once knew.

You see as great as he was on the field, John Mackey was even greater off the field. He was the president of the NFL Players Association for many years, and he was a pillar of strength. He stood up for himself, and even more impressively, he stood up for every one of his fellow players. He stood up to some very powerful NFL owners and sacrificed himself for the benefit of all of us. Mackey fought for the rights and riches that the multimillionaire players of today are enjoying. There's even some speculation that Mackey was denied being the first tight end in the Hall of Fame because he pissed off so many of the NFL brass in his fight for players' rights that they wanted to punish him in some way. I don't know about that, but I do know that life plays tricks on us all—both good and bad. His illness is a cruel trick on John Mackey. The things that Mackey stood for as a man, and the things he did for the benefit of every one of his NFL brothers, deserves a book of its own.

OZZIE NEWSOME
Cleveland Browns, 1978-1990

College: Alabama
Pro Bowls: 1982, 1985, 1986
Honors: Pro Football Hall of Fame, Class of 1999

Unlike Mackey, Newsome was *not* a typical tight end. His value as a receiver was enormous, and it far outstripped what he did as a blocker. Newsome could certainly block well, but he never wanted to really tee off on anybody. He was a precision blocker, and that was always good enough to keep me occupied so the Browns could get their sweep going.

BOB TRUMPY
Cincinnati Bengals 1968-1977
Colleges: Illinois, Utah
Pro Bowls: 1969, 1970, 1971, 1974

Trumpy was always getting in my way like a little Pekinese dog, nibbling at my feet. However, he was a six-foot-six, 230-pound little Pekinese dog. Then after the play, he'd throw out a smartass remark, especially if the Bengals got some yardage. Trumpy was one of those guys who'd try to get under your skin, like Chester, and he could mess your whole day up if you let him piss you off. Trumpy always got the job done, though, and he'd keep me tied up long enough for his offense to make something happen. What more could you ask for?

Offensive Linemen

BOB BROWN
Philadelphia Eagles, 1964-1968;
L.A. Rams, 1969-1970; Oakland Raiders, 1971-1973
College: Nebraska
Pro Bowls: 1966, 1967, 1968, 1970, 1971, 1972
Honors: Pro Football Hall of Fame, Class of 2004

Bob "Boomer" Brown *exploded* off the snap of the ball and right into anyone, or anything, that got in his way. There's no other way to describe it. He was just murder. He tossed players hither and yon like they were rag dolls. He would drive a guy right into the dirt, cover him over, and plant a cross over the grave.

We were preparing to play the Raiders in the early 1970s, and we watched the film Brown for the first time. He had this funny stance on the line with his leg sticking way out. It was weird, but it got the job done. Our other defensive end, Tody Smith, was scheduled to line up against Brown, but Smith had a sore toe. Somehow, I was talked into changing places with him, and I had to prepare to face Brown. Lucky me.

Speaking of luck, Smith's toe got better as the week went on, so I announced that he should probably take his job back, because I was feeling a little awkward playing at the other side. We played the Raiders that week, and I don't remember how badly Brown beat up on Smith, but it was a mismatch from the get-go. Brown just did in that game what he always did in every game—total domination.

DOUG DIEKEN
Cleveland Browns, 1971-1984

College: Illinois
Pro Bowls: 1980

Doug Dieken was a cheating, backstabbing, eye-poking, tripping, dirty, lowdown snake in the grass and a mean, rotten, vicious son of a bitch. He is also one of my best friends.

Dieken always swore that he never touched me on the field. His bodyguard was his linemate Henry Sheppard, whom I called the second dirtiest player in the NFL. The dirtiest, of course, was Dieken. Sheppard and Dieken would always try to clip me, and then we'd break into one of our classic fights. One time, I just said, "To hell with the play," and I started kicking the snot out of Dieken.

Dieken had great talent, and I loved playing against him, because he always brought it.

The juices were always flowing when we faced off. I never knew what he was going to do on the field, and that was exciting in a twisted way. If I was able to get past him on the line, I remembered to watch my back because Dieken was always ready to take someone from behind. I can't tell you how many times I had a clean shot at his quarterback, and then the next thing I knew my facemask is being pulled and I was going to the ground, courtesy of Mrs. Dieken's little Douglas. Then the flags flew, and the fight started. Yet, he'd still tell me it was all in my mind because he was not playing dirty.

After the final gunshot of every battle we fought, Dieken and I always hugged and put the game behind us. We never carried a grudge and never let anything on the field affect our friendship. In fact, when the Oilers threw a retirement party for me in 1983, I knew I had to have Dieken there. It really touched me that he made the trip down to Houston for that special night. So, just to summarize, Doug Dieken was a lowlife bastard, and he was, and will always be, one of my best buddies.

JOHN HANNAH
New England Patriots, 1973-1985

College: Alabama
Pro Bowls: 1977, 1979, 1980, 1981,
1982, 1983, 1984, 1985, 1986
Honors: NFL 75th Anniversary Team;
Pro Football Hall of Fame, Class of 1991

I may have gone from Trenton, New Jersey, to Canton, Ohio, but John Hannah went from Canton, Georgia, to Canton, Ohio. When he writes *his* book, I'll sell him the perfect title for it—*From Canton to Canton.*

What more can I say about an offensive lineman who was All-Pro 10 times and was named Offensive Lineman of the Year four times? Well, I can tell you that battling Hannah was like running into a brick wall. He was a dynamo. He seemed as tall as he was wide. He was massive and quick as hell. When we'd watch him in game films to prepare for the Patriots, we would just marvel at him. We always had our hands full with Hannah, and he did it all without holding, without any dirty shots, and with total class. Hannah just outright beat his defensive line opponents every time.

JON KOLB
Pittsburgh Steelers, 1969-1981
College: Oklahoma State

Kolb apparently never played in any Pro Bowls, although I was convinced he was an All-Pro for several years. Before you start feeling sorry for him, please remember that he won four Super Bowls with Pittsburgh, so I doubt he's lost any sleep about it.

Kolb and Dieken were two of my toughest assignments every season. We had to play Dieken's Browns and Kolb's Steelers twice each year because they were both in our division. That's four games every season where I know I'm going to have my hands full.

Kolb was about my size, which made our matchup very exciting. The adrenaline was always so high in those Steeler–Oiler games, and I particularly remember a *Monday Night Football* game against Pittsburgh in the Astrodome. I beat Jon Kolb for two back-to-back sacks on Terry Bradshaw. Beating a player of

Kolb's caliber on two consecutive plays, and on Monday night against our greatest rivals, was enough to make my year!

I had some great battles with Jon Kolb, and he gave me fits on a regular basis. It doesn't matter to me that he didn't play in any Pro Bowls—I've always thought he deserved more consideration for the Pro Football Hall of Fame. In the meantime, he's got four Super Bowl rings, and induction in my Smashmouth Hall of Fame, to console him.

LARRY LITTLE
San Diego Chargers, 1967-1968;
Miami Dolphins, 1969-1980
College: Bethune-Cookman
Pro Bowls: 1970, 1972, 1973, 1974, 1975
Honors: Pro Football Hall of Fame, Class of 1993

The awesome rushing attack of the 1970s Miami Dolphins was led by the blocking of Larry Little. He was a fantastic pass blocker, too, but he was such an intimidating force on the run. We're still close friends to this day, and one of his favorite gags is to tell me that I may have beaten him on a play once or twice, but I never got one of these—and then he holds up his hand to show off his Super Bowl ring from the Dolphins' perfect 1972 season. That's typical Larry Little—he was always a world-champion trash talker.

We played in some Pro Bowls together and got to be friends. I gave him the nickname "Mr. Buzzard" one year because of his eccentric eating habits. Little would order a full bucket of Kentucky Fried Chicken and then come into a room full of guys without offering any of his food to anybody. Then he'd lick every one of those chicken pieces so no one would snatch one away from him. As Little picked clean a wing or breast in the bucket, he threw the bones in the corner of the room. That's "Mr. Buzzard."

ANTHONY MUNOZ
Cincinnati Bengals, 1980-1992

College: USC

Pro Bowls: 1982, 1983, 1984, 1985, 1986, 1987, 1988, 1989, 1990, 1991, 1992

Honors: NFL 75th Anniversary Team; Pro Football Hall of Fame, Class of 1998

Yes, you read his stats correctly. Munoz went to the Pro Bowl in every one of his last 11 seasons. That's 11 out of 13 seasons. Munoz defined the position of offensive tackle. First, he protected Kenny Anderson's blindside on the left, because Anderson was a right-handed quarterback. Then, when left-handed Boomer Esiason came to the Bengals, Munoz was point man on all of the rushing plays to the left. Anthony Munoz was the perfect package.

We only played against each other in my last two years in the league, I'm sorry to say. The only way to beat Munoz was to get into him quick and try to collapse his arms. I learned another trick in dealing with Munoz from Jesse Baker, my replacement at defensive end on the Oilers. Baker suggested putting my helmet right into Munoz's chest and just pushing like hell.

I was blessed with quickness off the snap of the ball in my stance, so I'd try to outrun Munoz and get around him. No matter how many tricks and gimmicks you thought up to beat Munoz, there was never any guarantee that anything was going to work. No one could drive block like Munoz, and I'll always regret that I didn't have to face him more often to test myself against one of the very best.

ART SHELL
Oakland Raiders, 1968-1982

College: Maryland State–Eastern Shore
Pro Bowls: 1973, 1974, 1975, 1976, 1977, 1978, 1979, 1981
Honors: Pro Football Hall of Fame, Class of 1989

Even though I used to beat Art Shell regularly, I let him block me just a few times so he'd be able to make the Pro Football Hall of Fame. Seriously, though, Shell was a great blocker and a massive physical presence who used his size brilliantly. Once he got his hand out and grabbed you (even though he always swore he never held me), it was a hopeless cause.

Off the field, Shell has always been a prince of a guy. Our first battles on the football field were fought in college. Shell played for Maryland State, which was a main rival for us at North Carolina A&T. In fact, Shell's college coach was very mad at me for choosing A&T over Maryland State. His coach would urge Shell to knock me out of the game if possible. They ran every play at me to teach me a lesson. Ah, but I was too quick for them. I was like the Predator. They never knocked me out of a game.

Shell was so great as an offensive lineman that the only times I ever beat him were when I timed the snap of the ball just right. I always tried to outthink him in order to gain some kind of advantage against his incredible skills, but trying to outthink Art Shell on a football field is a fruitless endeavor.

JIM TYRER
Dallas Texans, 1961-1962;
Kansas City Chiefs, 1963-1973

College: Ohio State
Pro Bowls: 1963, 1964, 1965, 1966,
1967, 1969, 1970, 1971, 1972
Honors: All-Time AFL Team

How many players went to *nine* Pro Bowls and never made the Pro Football Hall of Fame? It seems impossible to imagine. Then again, Jim Tyrer is almost impossible to imagine.

He was a challenge, to be sure, but I always loved a challenge. The bigger my opponent, the harder I worked. I think I had some decent games against Tyrer, but once he got his hands on you, it was over. He'd overpower you with those gigantic mitts of his, and you were done.

♦ ♦ ♦ ♦ ♦

RAYFIELD WRIGHT
Dallas Cowboys, 1967-1979

College: Fort Valley State
Pro Bowls: 1972, 1973, 1974, 1975, 1976, 1977

Rayfield Wright was another big challenge, because his height and size made a real difference on the Cowboy offensive line. After you finished battling all six feet, six inches and 260 pounds of Rayfield Wright, Dallas had bought the much-needed extra two seconds to get their brilliant play-calling in motion. Wright was one of the league's premier run blockers for more than 10 years, and anyone who knows football knows that he should have been in the Pro Football Hall of Fame years ago.

The Punter

RAY GUY
Oakland/L.A. Raiders, 1973-1986

College: Southern Mississippi
Pro Bowls: 1974, 1975, 1976, 1977, 1978, 1979, 1981)
Honors: NFL 75th Anniversary Team

Location, location, location is not just the key to great real estate investment. It's the stock in trade for any great punter. Guy won several games for his Raiders by sticking his opponents with lousy field position. He made a difference, especially in the play-offs.

This boy kicked the ball, and we just sat and waited for it to come back down. I always pitied the receiver waiting for the ball on one of his punts, because Guy's hang time was interminable. He punted the ball so high at the Astrodome in one game that he hit a speaker.

I've never been one of those people who considered the kicking game to be secondary to offense and defense. Kicking is one-third of the game. A kicker, or a punter, is a football player as much as any player on the team. You can't win without them. If you don't have a great kicking game, you are missing a key element in the winning formula.

Ray Guy was the greatest NFL punter *ever.* If Ray Guy is not in the Pro Football Hall of Fame, then what's the Hall of Fame for anyway?

The Kicker

GEORGE BLANDA
Chicago Bears, 1949-1958;
Houston Oilers, 1960-1966;
Oakland Raiders, 1967-1975

College: Kentucky
Pro Bowls: 1962, 1963, 1964, 1968
Honors: Pro Football Hall of Fame, Class of 1981

The legend. Actually, Blanda is more than a legend. He's Mount Rushmore. Blanda played in 340 games over the course of more than 26 years and finally retired just short of his 49th birthday. No one will *ever* do any of that again.

Even though I never got to play against George Blanda as a quarterback, I saw him often enough as a placekicker. When Blanda lined up to kick a field goal, you could be sure it was going to be three points. It was money in the bank. That's a legend.

Head Coaches

CHUCK NOLL
Pittsburgh Steelers, 1969-1981

Won-Lost Record: 193-148 (.566 winning percentage)
Honors: Super Bowls IX, X, XIII, XIV;
Pro Football Hall of Fame, Class of 1993

Chuck Noll was my kind of coach. He enforced discipline, and he loved defensive players who were fast, strong, quick off the ball, and hard-hitting. He never sought the spotlight and always gave credit to his players. Most importantly, he won.

I played in a number of Pro Bowl games under Coach Noll, and I would have loved the chance to play for him on a regular basis. Just like Bum Phillips, Coach Noll knew his players' buttons and how best to push them. He had great awareness of the weapons at his disposal—Bradshaw, Harris, Lynn Swann, John Stallworth, Rocky Bleier, and "The Steel Curtain" defense—and he obviously knew how to get the most out of them.

We had enormous respect for Coach Noll on the Oilers, and I think he had respect for us. In fact, he gifted our entire team with Samsonite briefcases one season. We had just knocked his archrivals, the Cleveland Browns, out of the playoffs, and he wanted to show his appreciation. I'll never forget that, Chuck, but you really didn't have to, you know—it was entirely *our* pleasure!

HANK STRAM
Dallas Texans/Kansas City Chiefs, 1960-1974; New Orleans Saints, 1976-1977)

Won-Lost Record: 131-97 (.571 winning percentage)
Honors: 1962 & 1966 AFL Champs;
Super Bowl IV Champs;
Pro Football Hall of Fame, Class of 2003

I always loved watching the late great Hank Stram on the sidelines of a game so it was a special treat for me to be inducted in the same Pro Football Hall of Fame class with him. We became fast friends during that whirlwind Hall of Fame juggernaut in 2003. My wife, Pat, and I stayed very close to Coach Stram (and his delightful wife, Phyllis) right up until he passed away on July 4, 2005. There'll never be another Hank Stram.

Coach Stram was an innovator on both offense and defense. He engineered a two tight end offensive scheme that provided an extra blocker on the line and slowed down the pass rush long enough to give Dawson more time to connect with his wide receivers. He perfected the use of a nose tackle in both the 3-4 and 4-3 defensive line formations. "The Little General" was also a trash talker, but he always backed it up by winning—and winning—and winning.

He was really in his element at old Arrowhead Stadium. Arrowhead was located right on the street, so when the team bus pulled up to let us out, it was like driving right up to your own garage. We'd walk 10 yards off the bus, and there we were, right in the stadium. The fans were always crazy, and the atmosphere was electric. I'll never forget that the Chiefs had this brown and white horse named Paint who was ridden around the perimeter of the stadium every time Kansas City scored. Coach Stram beat us so badly in one game and they scored so frequently, that I was afraid that poor old Paint was going to faint from exhaustion.

I really love to watch those classic NFL films of Coach Stram prowling the sidelines during the Super Bowl. He was articulate, funny, flambuoyant, and a snappy dresser to boot. I'll never forget the picture of those giants on the Chiefs—guys like Ernie Ladd, Fred Williamson, Jim Tyrer, Ed Budde—all surrounding this little guy and listening intently for the game plan.

Hank Stram was a real showman. He carried his game plan in his hand, all rolled up for maximum slapping emphasis whenever something exciting happened. Coach Stram brought color and theatricality to the game. I'm proud that we went into the Pro Football Hall of Fame together.

Chapter 11

"IS THERE LIFE AFTER FOOTBALL?"

Hank Stram always did a wonderful job of preparing his Chief players for their lives after football. He used to say to them, "You are not football players. That's just what you do." Coach Stram's retired players seemed to be a successful, well-adjusted bunch of guys who must have taken his advice to heart. All professional athletes have to come to grips with how we will spend our lives after our playing careers are over. Because most athletes are retiring in the prime of their lives, long before middle age, we've got a lot of years to live after the cheering stops.

Starting in 1978, I worked an offseason job with Anheuser-Busch here in the Houston area. I was paired up with Robert Newhouse, the Dallas Cowboy running back, and we'd do promotions for Budweiser all around the country. Whenever a new wholesaler or big grocery chain was opening or whenever Budweiser sponsored a major concert, Newhouse and I went to sign autographs and press the flesh. Anheuser-Busch sent us both to its school to learn the ropes of the business, and they paid us about $20,000 to $25,000 for the offseason. It was just something to do. I didn't know at the time it was a career move. Newhouse and I got the gig thanks to Cal Weinstein, the events coordinator for the NFL Players Association. It was a great job, but I only saw it as an opportunity to do something a little different. I couldn't have imagined that I'd be retiring from Anheuser-Busch as a full-time employee 20 years later.

Ever since I moved to Houston from North Carolina on a year-round basis in 1971, I always had an offseason job. Until the Budweiser job started in 1978, I had spent the previous seven offseasons working for a big-and-tall men's store in Houston called Zindler's. For some reason, I became convinced that I was going to be a haberdasher when my playing days were over. Zindler's started me out on the floor as a salesman, but I had no idea what I was doing. I couldn't sell so much as a sock. I didn't like failing at anything, so I decided to apply my football training philosophy to haberdashery. I felt I needed to train hard, dedicate myself to learning, and prepare myself for the challenge. So I asked to be put in the basement to start learning the men's clothing business from the ground up—literally. There were long hours at Zindler's, and I learned an awful lot. Ultimately, though, the biggest lesson I learned was that the haberdasher's life was not for me. The Anheuser-Busch job came at just the right time.

Newhouse and I thrived in our promotion work for Budweiser. We started to think that what we really wanted to do was own distributorships so that became our incentive to work even harder for the company. Several other retired NFL players had been granted beer distributorships—Bob Lilly, Willie Davis, and Ben Davidson, to name a few—so we knew the precedent was there. After a few years, Newhouse decided to try another profession, but I stayed with Anheuser-Busch. After I retired from the Oilers in 1983, my first position with the company was as an area manager, where I coordinated community events and initiated sales to retailers. Later I moved on to be a marketing manager and learned all about the signage and the art of product placement. My last assignment with Anheuser-Busch was as director of government affairs for our region. I never got the distributorship that I had hoped to have, but the work was usually interesting, and the company generally treated me well.

After almost 10 years as a full-time Anheuser-Busch employee, I got the itch to work in football again. It was 1991, during Jack Pardee's tenure as head coach of the Oilers, and I got it in my head to get back into the game. I made an appointment with the Oilers' general manager, Mike Holovak, and I expressed an interest in coaching for the Houston Oilers. Instead he tried to steer me toward a semi-pro team, the San Antonio Toros. Holovak told me he didn't think I would really enjoy coaching because I had no coaching experience and *only* played in the league for 16 years. I won't pretend that it didn't hurt to be turned away like that. I wanted the chance to teach young players. One of my favorite parts of the last two seasons I played was that I served as a mentor and an unofficial teacher to some of the younger players. It's very common to see players retire from the league and then get a coaching job the very next season, usually for their former team. No such luck for me. It's still a sore topic.

My friends Kenny Houston and Garland Boyette have since assured me that it was probably just as well that I didn't get into pro coaching. They say that the long hours, the backstage politics, and the prima donna players would not have been for me. Still, I'll always wonder, "What if...?"

Actually, if I had ever become a head coach in the NFL, I'm sure I would have taken bits and pieces from every coach I had, all the way from high school to college to the pros. A little bit from here and a little bit from there. I would have distilled all of those different philosophies and coaching styles and ways of relating to players into my own particular style. These days I'm coaching on my grandson Devin's youth football team, and that's probably just right for me, actually. At least they can't talk back to me!

In 1995, I had been single for about three years and I had every intention of staying that way. After two divorces, I was in a self-searching mode and was fully expecting to live alone for the rest of my life. Eventually I healed from the last divorce, and then I allowed myself to actually think that I might meet someone to share my life with again. There were so many things that happened during my two marriages to make me distrustful and suspicious of falling into the same traps, but I was ready to take the plunge with the right woman. As it happened, Ms. Right was at the bank.

Pat Armelin was a lending assistant at my bank in the Medical Center, and we talked every time I went in to check on my account. After a few purely professional exchanges, I began to feel some sparks starting to fly. I was drawn to her earthiness, her kindness, her openness, and her no-frills tastes. Pat is decidedly not high maintenance and she is not a night person—two big pluses with me. She is what my father would have called a down-home country gal. In fact, Pat possesses some of my mother's very best qualities—great concern for other people, a strong faith, and a commitment to help anyone in need. We shared simple tastes, and we had both been through rough times in our previous marriages. Most importantly, we really had chemistry together.

Pat has a great head on her shoulders. Her organizational skills and her take-charge personality were just what I needed around the house, too. If I were writing a prescription for the perfect woman with whom to spend my life, Pat would fit it perfectly. We laugh a lot, we fish a lot, and we enjoy all of the simple pleasures that make life so special. Places like Hawaii and Las Vegas are a lot of fun for us, but you know you've found the right person for you when they even enjoy going to Snow Hill, Maryland, with you. It may have taken me three tries, but I finally got this marriage thing right!

I got another football itch in 1999. There were so many fantastic people working at Anheuser-Busch, but there were some rotten ones, too. The rotten ones were beginning to wear me down, and I got the idea, against the advice of many of my coworkers, to quit the company before retirement and try something else for a few years. It's no coincidence that this idea came to me upon the arrival of Houston's new NFL franchise—The Texans. I went to the Houston Texans offices for a two-hour meeting with their general manager, Charlie Caserly. He was just as negative as Mike Holovak had been about the prospect of my return to the league. I wasn't even looking for a coaching job this time, though. I wanted to use my marketing skills and business experience, plus my access to the movers and shakers in the

Houston area, to do some work in player development. Billy "White Shoes" Johnson was having great success in a similar job with the Atlanta Falcons, and I felt that my connections to the mayor of Houston, the chief of the police, and even the governor's office would all serve me well in a job like that. It would be a chance to help young players adjust to life in the NFL. I could have helped them navigate the process of purchasing their first home, getting them settled into the community with their families, and generally guiding them through the treacherous waters of professional sports. The modern-day rookie may be entering the league as a millionaire, but he's still a youngster in many ways, and he's going to have 50 to 60 years of living to do after he retires from football. As Coach Stram made so clear, it's important to lay the groundwork for your life, not just for the few short years of mega-paychecks. Very few players get to play for 16 years in the NFL—I was lucky. So, my proposal to Caserly was to be given the opportunity to help young players prepare for their football life and then life after football. I waited to hear from Caserly before I proceeded with my plans to leave Anheuser-Busch—I'm still waiting.

My parents were in failing health in the late 1990s. My father had mellowed considerably as he got older. He had never come to any games during my life, but no matter how tough he was, we always knew he loved us. He had encouraged me to stay in college because he didn't want me to have to do the back-breaking work that filled almost every day of his adult life. I knew he was proud of my accomplishments in the NFL because he'd be sure to tell everyone who I was and what I did whenever I visited his job sites. Diabetes had taken his eyesight and both of his legs, but he stayed surprisingly chipper. Whenever he was asked how he was feeling, the answer was always the same—"Peachy!"

As he got older and sicker, my father started believing every home remedy and quack doctor's theory on restoring his health.

Someone had told him that drinking a little turpentine every day would bring back his eyesight so he started adding a little of it to his morning cereal. My father finally passed away in 1999, and my sainted mother followed him in 2001. It still makes me emotional to think about the sacrifices they made for me, and all my brothers and sisters, to give us better lives than the ones they had. I still miss them both every day.

Life after football was, for me, like anybody else's life. I went to work and did my job, I took vacations; I spent time with my family and friends. There were plenty of joys, thanks to Pat, my three children, and my two grandchildren. There were sorrows, too, with the passing of my beloved parents. However, I couldn't have dreamed that the greatest personal and professional thrill of my life was still ahead.

Chapter 12

...TO CANTON

During my playing days, I don't ever remember being aware of the Pro Football Hall of Fame. I must have known that it was there, because we played in a Hall of Fame game against the Los Angeles Rams in 1971. It's just that I didn't really know what it was and what it meant to be enshrined there. I had probably even seen the televised induction ceremonies over the years, but how could I possibly identify with names such as Sammy Baugh, Red Grange, Jim Thorpe, Jim Brown, Dick "Night Train" Lane, Chuck Bednarik, etc., when I heard about their enshrinement? Those players were gods, not regular players like me. It just never even appeared on my personal radar. How could I ever dare to connect the concept of the Hall of Fame with my own playing career? I played football as hard, fast, and wide as I could, but I never thought that playing in the NFL would take me anywhere beyond a paycheck and a few good business contacts after I retired from the league.

Because I played in a lackluster media market like Houston, where our team was so bad for so long, it wasn't until years after I stopped playing that people began to talk about me in terms of the Hall of Fame. When my contemporaries in the NFL started getting inducted every year, I just assumed that the Hall of Fame was only for the winners. It was for the Steelers, the Cowboys, the Dolphins, and so on. It was for Terry Bradshaw, Joe Greene, Franco Harris, Jack Ham, Jack Lambert, Mike Webster, Roger Staubach, Bob Lilly, Tony Dorsett, Mel Renfro, Randy White, Bob Griese, Larry Csonka, Larry Little, Jim Langer, and Paul Warfield.

This is not false modesty. I honestly didn't think I was a Hall of Fame-caliber player compared to the guys who were getting in. Did the Hall of Fame voters even notice defensive linemen? Even if they did, they certainly wouldn't notice a lineman from a losing team in a city that never got any national media attention. To this day, I'm shocked and humbled that I was inducted. To permanently reside in the same Hall of Fame with someone such as Deacon Jones, whom I admired so much, is beyond my comprehension. I just can't help but ask, "Was I really that good?"

One day in 1998 my good friend Mark Adams came up with the idea to start a campaign calling for my Hall of Fame induction. To be honest, I just didn't believe it would really ever happen. I reasoned that I had already been eligible for induction since 1988, and if the voters didn't put me in after 10 years, why would they be inspired to do so now? However, he began researching my career and the careers of other defensive ends, and he prepared a letter to send to every Hall of Fame voter, which he felt would point out the very best arguments in support of my candidacy, and he faxed it to me.

I looked at it and began to read.

"Elvin Bethea played at defensive end for 16 seasons and in 210 games from 1968 to 1983. *No defensive end played in more games at this position!*

"Elvin Bethea played in eight Pro Bowls as defensive end in the 1970s. *No other defensive end went to more Pro Bowls in that decade! The only players who went to more Pro Bowls in the 1970s were Ken Houston, Alan Page, and Joe Greene!*

"Gino Marchetti is generally regarded as the NFL defensive end by whom all others are judged. *Gino Marchetti is the only Hall of Fame defensive end who has gone to more Pro Bowls than Elvin Bethea!*"

I looked at the paper in amazement. One thought kept echoing in the back of mind as I read and reread those words, "Was I really *that* good?!?"

"Wow," I thought to myself. "These can't be right."

After that letter went out to the Hall of Fame voters, my name began to appear on the list of nominees for Hall of Fame induction. The annual list of preliminary nominees is usually about 70 to 80 names long before it gets reduced to 15 finalists.

Then the voters meet on the day before the Super Bowl to elect the four to seven inductees to receive the ultimate honor. Once I began to appear on the preliminary list of nominees, I got interested in tracking who was elected every year. In 2003, I finally cracked the lineup and was chosen as one of the 15 finalists for induction, but I still refused to let myself believe it would ever happen.

By this time Mark now had an additional ally in this process—my old buddy John McClain, the sportswriter for the *Houston Chronicle.* It fell to McClain to speak on my behalf when the Hall of Fame voters convened to elect the Pro Football Hall of Fame Class of 2003. McClain told me that he took Mark's list of stats about me, photocopied them, and placed a copy in front of every chair at the writer's meeting. McClain said later that those stats really surprised and impressed the writers and that they made the difference in my eventual induction. Even when the big day of the election announcement came, I felt about as likely to be put in the Hall of Fame as I was to fly to Mars.

The officials at the Hall of Fame always advise the finalists to stay near the phone on Election Day. They sent a letter saying, "If you are one of the inductees, here are your tickets for Hawaii for the official introduction of the Class of 2003 at the Pro Bowl." Everyone I ran into for the previous two weeks would speak with enormous confidence about my chances for induction. Co-workers, family members, friends, and even strangers would tell me, "You are definitely going to make it." I've had enough setbacks in my life that I've sort of developed a more negative outlook on these things. I was convinced that I was poised to be handed yet another disappointment, so I just tried to prepare for the inevitable letdown.

The big day arrived, and I woke up at 8 a.m. The call from the Hall of Fame, if it was going to come, was supposed to happen around 3 p.m. Central time. I started staring at the clock around noon and began to count the minutes. It finally got to 3 p.m.

The phone rang.

I jumped out of my skin.

"Could this be it?" I thought as went to pick up the receiver.

I answered very tentatively, "Hello?"

"Elvin, it's Bob Hyde."

It wasn't Canton. It was my good friend, who had been with the Houston Oilers, and now the Tennessee Titans, for years.

"Don't call, Bob!" I yelled. "You scared me half to death!"

"I have something to tell you," he said.

Hyde reported that he had an inside source at the voter's meeting. He said that the writers were still deliberating, and, therefore, any calls from the Hall were going to be delayed. I thanked him for the scoop and hung up.

Then the phone calls started to come in from all over the country, and I had to tell every single caller that I was still waiting. Hyde still called regularly with updates, but I finally had to beg him not to call unless he had something concrete to report about the announcement. By this time my nerves were shot.

Another long hour crept by at an excruciatingly slow pace. Then the phone rang. It was Hyde.

"Are your bags packed?" he said.

I couldn't respond.

"You're in," he said after the silence.

I didn't know whether to cry or cheer. The swirl of emotions was especially confusing because this was not the official call from the Hall of Fame. I trusted Hyde, but he was actually only reporting secondhand information from his inside source. He got off the phone to let me keep the line open for the official word from Canton.

"Be sure to act surprised," he added before signing off.

Five minutes later, the phone rang again. The caller ID on the answering machine indicated "Pro Football Hall of Fame."

I picked up.

"Hello, Elvin. This is John Bankert, executive director of the Pro Football Hall of Fame. Congratulations. You are now one of the five members of the Class of 2003."

My wife Pat began jumping up and down and dancing around the bed. With all of that going on, I could think of only one thing to say.

"Thank you."

The rest of the day was nonstop phone calls. I talked to Bum Phillips and to reporters from all over the country. I don't remember which organizations I talked to or what I was asked. I heard from former teammates and even my boss at Anheuser-Busch headquarters in St. Louis.

The first person to appear at our door after the announcement was made public was Mark Berman, one of Houston's premier television sports directors. We had been friends for a long time, so I gave him the scoop with my first TV interview as a newly elected member of the Pro Football Hall of Fame.

By the way, I was in some excellent company in the Hall of Fame's Class of 2003. I was going in with Marcus Allen, Joe DeLamielleure, James Lofton, and Hank Stram. If it's true that people are really judged by the company they keep, then I was in great shape! Later that night when the whirlwind of emotions finally settled and I realized what it all meant, I broke down and cried.

January 2003. The Pro Football Hall of Fame Class of 2003 meets for the the first time at the Pro Bowl in Honolulu. From left: my wife, Pat; Marcus Allen; Phyllis and Hank Stram; Joe and Gerri DeLamielleure; and Beverly and James Lofton. **Photo courtesy of Elvin Bethea**

The next six months were crazy. It was a surreal period in my life. Everyone suddenly knew who I was now. I received phone calls from radio stations all around the country. There were calls from my alma mater in North Carolina and from my hometown of Trenton. People called from virtually every NFL city. I was just so happy to finally be in demand that I said yes to everything.

"Just tell me where you want me to go and when to be there," I told them.

I accepted every speaking engagement, every autograph show, and every charity appearance. After six months Pat came to the rescue because I was overextending myself and booking far too many engagements. Dates were starting to overlap so she got the whole mess in order for me. Mark took over the job of fielding offers for personal appearances and autograph shows so I nicknamed him "The Cheese Man." He got the name because these gigs came with the always welcomed monetary sustenance, which we called *cheese*. Income taxes are *government cheese*.

It was an unforgettable time. I saved every e-mail that I received during that time, and I put them into a folder to keep forever. I also used some of the time during those six months to prepare my acceptance speech for induction day. It didn't take long for me to choose the person I wanted to introduce me, however. I knew it just had to be coach Hornsby Howell from North Carolina A&T State. My parents may have raised me, but Coach Howell made me the person I am today, and he certainly made me into the football player I became. He gave me all of the tools and the work ethic that got me to the point where I was now being inducted into the Pro Football Hall of Fame. As a high school football player, I was probably above average, but Coach Howell pushed me to reach my maximum potential. He pushed me to the edge—and then over the edge.

When our plane landed in Cleveland in early August 2003, the Hall of Fame weekend was just getting started. I felt like a superstar—I had gone from a nobody to a celebrity in just six short months. When my family and I got off the plane and entered the terminal, I started signing autographs. As I bounced from one fan to the next, Bob McCarthy, the Hall of Fame volunteer who was assigned to escort us to Canton, came up to my party.

"We can't stop for anything here in the airport," McCarthy instructed as he ushered us away from the gate. "We can't stop for autographs or photographs or anything. We have to get to the car."

If he hadn't been there to keep us on task, I would probably have signed autographs for hours in that airport. McCarthy announced that my family would be making the hour-long drive to Canton in a van, but that Pat and I were going in our own vehicle. Just then, a Jaguar pulled up to the curb. A Jaguar! I'd never been in a Jaguar in my life.

"Most Hall of Famers get a Lincoln Continental, but you get a Jaguar," McCarthy explained as I eyed the beautiful piece of machinery.

Even if he was just flattering me, it still felt wonderful to believe it could be true! For someone who is used to hailing a cab at the airport, the Jaguar made me feel pretty special.

We got to our hotel in Canton and were given an itinerary for the weekend. There were occasional free moments set aside for breathing and intermittent visits to the bathroom, but otherwise every second was filled.

"We've got to stay on schedule," McCarthy cautioned throughout the weekend.

I just kept pinching myself. I couldn't believe everything that was going on around me. I'll never forget entering a room to attend a luncheon with my fellow Hall of Famers and then being awestruck by the faces that greeted me. Because 2003 marked the 40th anniversary of the first induction class in 1963, every living Hall of Famer had been invited back to the festivities of induction weekend as guests of the hall and about 140 Hall of Famers came, which was twice the usual turnout for an induction weekend. There was Dick Butkus, Bob Lilly, Frank Gifford, Chuck Bednarik, Deacon Jones, Forrest Gregg, Lenny Moore, Art Donovan, Raymond Berry, Joe Namath, Gino Marchetti, Mike Ditka, Joe Greene, Jim Ringo, Dante Lavelli, Lou Creekmur, Yale Lary, Joe Schmidt, Willie Davis, Willie Wood, Bobby Bell, Willie Lanier, Bob Griese, Ted Hendricks, Charley Trippi, "Bullet Bill" Dudley, and on and on and on. That luncheon made me wish I collected autographs. It was a moment I couldn't even have dreamed of. It was just indescribable to look around that room and feel like I belonged with these great players. Their names normally were spoken in hushed tones with incredible respect, and here they were in the room with me. It was too much to fathom.

On the evening before our actual induction ceremony on Sunday afternoon, Canton's mayor hosted the Mayor's Civic Dinner. This was the biggest, and probably the most emotional, of the weekend's festivities. It was held in the large civic arena in downtown Canton, and about 10,000 guests were in attendance. This was where the formal presentation of the famous gold Hall of Fame jackets was held for all of the new inductees. After each new inductee was given his gold jacket, and received some overwhelming love from that huge crowd, we lined up on the arena's center platform, surrounded on all sides by audience. Then the returning Hall of Famers were introduced one by one. As each returning Hall of Famer was introduced, he came up a ramp on one side of the stage, greeted each new member in the line, and then exited down the other side. It was the highlight of the entire weekend for me. I could never put into words how it felt to hear each of 140 names read out loud and then to be embraced so warmly by each one as they welcomed the five of us to this incredibly exclusive club. I can't speak for Allen, DeLamielleure, Lofton, or Coach Stram, but that magical night in the Canton Civic Center ranks as an even bigger thrill for me than the induction the next afternoon. And that's really saying something!

Much of the actual Induction Day is a big blur to me. I'm grateful to have the transcripts of the speeches made by all of the inductees and their presenters. I'm really happy to have a videotape of the ESPN broadcast of the induction, too. Without these, I don't think I'd have any way of clearly remembering anything that happened.

Sunday, August 3, 2003, began as a rainy day in Canton. The returning Hall of Famers, the new inductees, and their presenters were all protected under a covered stage situated at one end zone of the Hall of Fame's Fawcett Stadium. Every one of the several thousand spectators, however, was vulnerable to the elements—the rain, sweltering heat, harsh sun, etc. Cheap but functional rain slickers were distributed to the spectators, but it didn't do much in the way of proper protection. The sun did eventually poke through to make for a lovely day, but the hour or so of rain left everyone looking like they lost a massive water balloon fight.

After the introduction of the returning Hall of Famers and then the introduction of the Class of 2003, I found out that a surprise had been planned for me. My family and friends had been keeping a big secret for several weeks, and it came off without a hitch. During the singing of the national anthem, there was a dramatic flyover by some F-16 fighters that gave a tremendous resonance to the whole experience. Chris Berman, hosting the ceremonies for ESPN, announced a bit later that my son, LaMonte, was leading that flyover with a few of his fellow pilots. Then, LaMonte came out on stage in his flight suit and received a rousing ovation from the crowd as we shared an emotional

August 3, 2003. Induction Day was rainy and sunny, but the weather couldn't touch how sweet it was for me. **Pro Football Hall of Fame**

embrace. I had no idea he was going to do that, and it was just another surreal moment in a long series of surreal moments that began with the phone call from John Bankert in January.

Coach Stram was too ill for a live delivery of his acceptance speech, so he had recorded one on tape several weeks earlier. After Lenny Dawson presented Coach Stram for induction in the Hall, they played a funny, but powerfully moving video montage while Coach's distinctive voice filled the stadium. He ended the speech with such a touching tribute to his love for his wife, Phyllis, that there wasn't a dry eye in the house.

Now it was my turn. Chris Berman introduced my presenter, Hornsby Howell.

Coach Howell made his way to the podium and a flood of memories from our days at North Carolina A&T washed over me. He got to the podium and began to speak.

As Elvin Bethea's former football coach, I feel honored to be here on this momentous occasion before football's greatest to introduce him. Elvin has demonstrated that he's not only a talented football player, but he's also a leader on and off the field. Because he was selected for this distinguished honor, it fills my heart with joy and pride.

I reflect back to the summer of 1964 when a humble but confident young man named Elvin Bethea arrived on the campus of North Carolina A&T State University to play for me. He would often say, "Coach, I'm the best offensive lineman you ever had." I put up with it for one year. And then the next year, we were playing Tennessee State, and there was a lineman at Tennessee State who's a darn good defensive lineman—Claude Humphrey. Claude Humphrey and Elvin Bethea had a big battle, with Elvin as an offensive lineman. After the game, I wrote Claude a nice little note, "Thank you very much." And so, from then on, Elvin was a defensive player.

My lifelong mentor and football coach at North Carolina A&T State, Hornsby Howell, presented me for induction. I have never been happier. **Pro Football Hall of Fame**

Even as a first-year student in college, Elvin possessed tremendous work ethics. Even though no one was watching, you could always find him doing the little extra, trying to improve his craft, constantly trying to make himself better, making the sacrifices for the team.

After graduation from North Carolina A&T in 1968, Elvin was drafted by the Houston Oilers and played 16 years for them. [His] streak of 135 consecutive games played still stands as a club record. Elvin also holds Oiler records for the most games played— 210; most seasons played; most Pro Bowl appearances; Elvin led the team in quarterback sacks six times, including a career mark of 14.5 in 1976.

Elvin's quality of good character, integrity, talent, and solid work ethics are qualities I observed in him in1964. To his credit, these qualities have helped make him the man he is today. Often I have heard that football makes men out of boys, that it makes one a better person. I would also like to add that football makes great people like Elvin Bethea who has given to the game, fought through adversity, and given back to others.

Elvin, the honors you are receiving, and have received, are well deserved. It is a compliment to you for the past but also reflects the future of great football.

Ladies and gentlemen, Elvin Bethea.

I stepped to the podium and drank in the deafening cheers of the crowd. I really hadn't experienced that intoxicating sound since I retired 20 years earlier. After hugging Coach Howell, I began to speak. Apparently I went beyond my allotted seven minutes, but I had no sense of time while I was up there. I began by thanking the Hall of Fame Selection Committee, John Bankert and his staff, and the great city of Canton. I also told some of the stories about my high school coach, Pat Clements. Then I gave a good long section to honor Coach Howell for his invaluable impact on my life and career. I continued with further reflection.

"This is the greatest day for me ever... My family, friends, and fellow Hall of Famers, before you stands a very humble person who never thought it possible that such a day as this would ever come. Like every man with whom I share this stage, I didn't make it here on my own. Looking back on my life, I remember many people whose shoulders I stood on and the people who pushed me through and pushed me forward to become the person I am today. Through their guidance, inspiration, motivation, and discipline, I have now achieved the ultimate accomplishment of my football career."

I spoke about my favorite coaches in the pros, Sid Gillman and especially Bum Phillips. I thanked Eddie Biles for my final year in the NFL. It was great to know that Coach Biles was in the audience at the induction, along with my favorite teammate, Dan Pastorini. I had to thank Bud Adams, too, because I was very proud to be standing on that stage as a Houston Oiler. There were only three of us in the Hall of Fame who played the majority of our careers in Houston—Earl Campbell, Mike Munchak, and myself. Then I came to the fans, my friends, and my family.

"Fans of Houston, I know you're watching me out there. You're the greatest. I have to mention those 1978 and 1979 teams where we took second place to the Pittsburgh Steelers. But the only thing, once we got back to our Astrodome, we had 60,000 people waiting for us. That was the greatest feeling that I had ever had while playing for the Houston Oilers. Thank you, fans.

"I'd like to John McClain, who was our sportswriter, who was my champion as far as really working hard to get me on this stage.

"Mr. Bob Hyde, who was a real friend of mine. It goes back to the Oiler days. He kept in touch with me and let me know where I stood as far as getting here today. Thank you, Bob.

"Mr. Mark Adams—I call him 'The Cheese Man.' Mark is a guy who found out many stats on me that I didn't know, and he sent them to the selection committee many times over the years. And, finally we got here, Mark. Thank you.

"All of my relatives, who are here, quite a few of them drove many miles from New Jersey, Florida, and California. I thank you. I hope I make you proud for this day and many more.

"LaMonte, my oldest son, who surprised me—I knew he was a pilot, but I didn't know he was going to be flying over today. He's made me proud, very proud.

"Brittany, my daughter, I hope you are as proud of me today as I am of you. She is now working with Child Protective Services in Houston, and she's going to be very successful in her life.

"And Damon, who's my youngest, I would like to say I'm very proud of him. We are hoping he can get a shot at pro football, and he's been working even harder than I ever worked. Damon, I just say, 'Keep your eyes on the sky, keep your eyes on the pride, keep everything together, and you're going to make it.'

"Pat, my wife, I thank you because of all your hard work over the years watching over me, and sticking beside me. Every time I ask her, 'Should I do this?' Pat always supports me in every way, in every matter. I thank you for today."

Then came the tough stuff. I was confident that I could get through the entire speech without breaking down. I was sure that I'd be able to hold it together. Pat and my sister Darlene were not so sure, however. When I began to pay tribute to my parents, I was overcome with emotion. It sunk in that they were not physically there. In one fell swoop, I realized just how much they had meant to me, in every aspect of my life, and now they were not there to share in the culmination of all my professional achievements. At one point in this section, I just had to stop to collect myself. It was difficult to continue. I heard some cheers of encouragement from the crowd, and, somehow, I got through it.

"My mother and father are not here today, but all the times that they gave me, all the good times. All the times that I remem-

My family shared the Hall of Fame experience with me. We were still drying out from the rainstorm when this picture was taken. From left: my youngest son, Damon Bethea; my oldest son, Lt. JG LaMonte Bethea; my granddaughter, Sydney; my sister, Darlene Bethea-Chester; my nephew, Torray Chester; my wife; me; my grandson, Devin, and my daughter, Brittany. **Pro Football Hall of Fame**

ber my mother or father picking me up from practice, whether it was cold or hot. I wish my mother was here, to just see her smile. I'm sure they're smiling on me today—both my mother and father.

"My father was very tough. He gave me the toughness I have. He always worked, and that's all he did and that's what he thought I should have done. My parents were the ones who really stayed behind me, pushed me to where I am today. My strength comes from them.

"My mother was very religious. There was a song that she loved. It was about God and how you should just follow His lead. The song went, 'God—He may not come when you want Him, but He's always on time.' And I'd like to say, thank you to the Hall of Fame. Thank you, my fellow Hall of Famers. Today is definitely on time."

And so, it was over. What a day! What a weekend! What a year! What a life!

It was as though my life was like Christmas morning and I was a kid again—with one distinct difference: There was nothing missing. It was as though all of the great friends and fans I've made in my football career were a Christmas tree, and those unforgettable AFC championship games against Pittsburgh in 1978 and 1979 were the tinsel and the ornaments decorating it. The Hall of Fame, however, was the final, glorious cap to it all. It was the star on top of the Christmas tree—the pinnacle. It just couldn't get higher than that.

Someone pointed out to me in 2003, during all that Hall of Fame hoopla, that there were only 181 players who have been inducted into the Hall of Fame over the years. That's only about 200 players out of the 18,000 or so who have played in the NFL over its 80-plus-year history. I'm one of those elite few now. The membership grows by only a very little bit each year. These 181 were all absolutely and unequivocally fantastic players, so I can't fully accept what that must say about me and my career as a professional football player. It always comes back to the same question for me—Was I really *that* good?

Celebrate the Variety of American and Texas Sports
in These Other Releases from Sports Publishing!

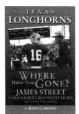

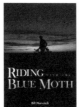

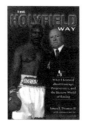